SHIRLEY WATTS'

FLOWERS
in CROSS STITCH

Shirley Watts'
FLOWERS
in CROSS STITCH

MEREHURST

FOR MY BROTHER, KEN, WHOSE ENCOURAGEMENT MEANS SO MUCH TO ME

Published in 1995 by Merehurst Limited
Ferry House, 51-57 Lacy Road, Putney, London SW15 1PR

ISBN 1 85391 427 4

Edited by Heather Dewhurst

Photography by Di Lewis, except for the pictures on pages 5, 6, 7, 10–14, 26, 30–34, 40, 46–48, 66, 68, 70, 86, 88, 94–96, 99, 105, 114 and 115, which were provided by Shirley Watts, and the pictures on pages 75, 77, 83, 109, 116 and 119 which are copyright © Harry Smith Agency
Illustrations by King & King Design Associates
Colour separation by P. & W. Graphics Pte Ltd
Printed in Singapore by C.S. Graphics Pte

CONTENTS

Introduction 6

ℐ NTRODUCTION

FLOWERS HAVE A UNIVERSAL APPEAL. Small children cannot resist the large golden heads of the ubiquitous dandelion, and nimble-fingered youngsters, even in this age of advanced technology, still experience pleasure as they make daisy chains in the time-honoured way. Flowers decorate our homes, our churches and many of our public buildings, and they bring colour to our gardens, greenhouses, parks and public places. In the countryside a cornfield red with poppies, a woodland carpeted with bluebells, or a grassy bank yellow with wild daffodils cannot fail to delight the eye. When we are sick or depressed, flowers help to lift our spirits, and at all the happiest times of our lives flowers never fail to enhance the occasion. From the toddler

clutching his bunch of limp dandelions, to the pensioner proudly tending his allotment stocked with prize-worthy chrysanthemums, everyone feels uplifted by the colour, the perfume, the delicacy and the sheer magic of flowers.

FAVOURITE FLOWERS

As I am writing this, the first flowers of the new year are brightening the grey, water-logged expanse of our garden. The brave winter jasmine with its fragile yellow flowers cascades from the wall of the porch. It has flowered continuously since the late autumn. Delicate snowdrops nod submissively in the face of icy gusts of wind, and the species crocuses poke through the cold sodden lawn, opening their petals wide like jewels in the brief periods of winter sunshine. By the front door, sheltered from the worst of the weather, red, yellow and cream primulas bring a promise that spring will soon be with us again. These first flowers of the year are to me the most precious of all because, as they have done from time immemorial, they bear witness to the reawakening of the earth once more.

It was these early spring flowers that I missed most when I lived for a time in the tropics. In Jamaica, many of the flowers were vividly coloured, flamboyant and, for me, they were truly spectacular. The flame colour of the poinciana blossom, the large red heads of the poinsettias, the scarlet, salmon pink and yellow hibiscus flowers, the purple and pink bougainvillea, the deep

Auricula (Primula auricula)

golden day lilies, the sky-blue plumbago
and the deep orange-red of the ground
orchids each provided a colourful display in
its season. There were also smaller and
more delicate flowers, but they were over-
shadowed by the more eye-catching blooms.

In choosing the flowers for this book, I
have selected a wide variety in the hope of
including something to appeal to everyone.
There are wild flowers and cultivated
blooms, flowers from high altitudes and
flowers from the humid tropics of low lati-
tudes. There are flowers which are colourful
and decorative, and there are some of the
more diminutive ones with culinary or
medicinal properties. All, I hope, are ones
which the flower-lover will enjoy.

Crocus sp.

Each chapter has its own theme and
includes one or more projects, but with a
little imagination the designs can be used in
a variety of ways. Worked on different
counts and on different coloured evenweave backgrounds, the designs can be used
to decorate a much wider range of articles
than there would be space to illustrate in
the pages of a single book. I hope that you
will enjoy working these designs. Use my
ideas as a spring-board from which you can
launch yourself into a host of projects from
your own imagination. Above all, have fun
with your stitching and, in turn, it will give
pleasure to those around you.

Chapter One

As Time Goes By

TIME GOVERNS ALL OUR LIVES, and calendars, almanacks and clocks are all methods we use to keep track of time. Time is inextricably linked with the movement of the earth and the moon in relation to the sun. A day is the time it takes for the earth to revolve once upon its own axis – a little less than 24 hours. A month is the time between two new moons. A lunar month is about 29½ days. A year is the time taken by the earth to travel around the sun – 365 days, 5 hours, 48 minutes and 46 seconds. Since none of these times adds up to round numbers, and because the lunar months do not fit exactly into the solar year, the business of devising a workable calendar which did not require correction at regular intervals to bring it back into line with the actual seasons, exercised the minds of scholars for centuries.

DEVISING CALENDARS

The Egyptians, around 4200BC, were the first to measure a year's length with a fair degree of accuracy. The Babylonians, over 1,000 years later, devised a calendar with 12 lunar months, but the year had only 354 days. After a few years, the spring months occurred in the winter of the actual year, and when this happened they had to add in an extra month to bring the calendar back into line with the actual seasons!

Our present calendar is based on the Julian Calendar, worked out by Julius Caesar. It implemented leap years every fourth year to accommodate the odd quarter day but, in spite of this, the calendar was approximately 11 minutes longer than the actual year. Eleven minutes per year, however, accumulated into ten days by the 16th century. Easter and other church festivals were all out of season, and Pope Gregory X111 decreed that ten days should be removed from the year 1582. Great Britain continued to use the old Julian Calendar until 1752, by which time the error had increased to 11 days. To correct this, in 1752, the 14th September was the day after the 2nd September. Imagine the anger and confusion as people believed that they had lost 11 days of their lives!

ALMANACK SAMPLER

Only 35 years after that memorable year, a girl named Elizabeth Knowles worked what I believe to be a most intriguing almanack sampler. Elizabeth's sampler begins with the year 1787 and goes through to 1847. Given

Lords-and-ladies (Arum maculatum)

any date, you can work out the day of the week on which that date occurred. If, for example, I had been born on the 31st January 1840, from Elizabeth's almanack I can work out that I would have been born on a Saturday. When I first discovered this sampler, I wondered who had originally worked out the almanack, and I was fascinated with the possibility of working out a similar one for the present century.

One thing puzzled me. Elizabeth had allowed a space before each leap year as you would expect, to make the adjustment for the extra day, but there was no leap year for 1800. Was this, I asked myself, an oversight, or was there some reason for the omission? I discovered that in making adjustments to keep the new Gregorian Calendar correct for the future, Pope Gregory had decreed that leap year should be left out in the last year of every century, except where the number of that year was divisible by 400. The year 1800 was, therefore, not a leap year, but at the end of our present century, the year 2000 *will* be a leap year.

MODERN ALMANACK

Elizabeth Knowles' almanack is decorated with birds, trees and flowers. For my modern almanack, I decided that it would be appropriate to design 12 wild flowers, each one representing a month of the year, with the spring and summer seasons above the almanack and autumn and winter below. For March I chose the delicate white wood anemone (*Anemone nemorosa*), a plant that, as its name suggests, grows in deciduous woodland and flowers before the trees come into leaf. I remember being thrilled to see it flowering in great profusion along the grass verges one early spring.

For April I chose the purple greater butterwort (*Pinguicula grandiflora*) which likes growing in boggy conditions. Its curled, sticky leaves ensnare small flies which are digested by the plant, providing nutrients lacking in the soil.

May is represented by lords-and-ladies (*Arum maculatum*), a strange plant where the tiny flowers are hidden at the base of a poker-like stalk, partly enclosed by the yellow-green hood. I always look for these plants when on holiday in Dorset. They grow freely in the shade of the high hedges that line a narrow footpath down to the beach at Charmouth.

For June I chose the scarlet pimpernel (*Anagallis arvensis*), one of the very few truly scarlet flowers growing wild in Northern Europe. I thought it an appropriate flower for a project on time, since it is used by country people to tell the time as well as to forecast the weather. It opens about 8am and closes up about 3pm, unless rain threatens, in which case it closes earlier.

The creeping bellflower (*Campanula rapunculoides*) with its beautiful blue petals, fused along part of their length to form a bell-shape, represents July. The large, yellow, sunny flower of the evening primrose (*Oenothera erythrosepala*), introduced from North America, represents August and completes the spring-summer flowers.

Along the lower border of the almanack, autumn begins with heather (*Calluna vulgaris*) for September. I love to be in Scotland in autumn when the heather carpets the moorland and mountains for as far as the eye can see.

By October wild flowers are becoming scarce, but thrift (*Armeria maritima*), growing in dense clumps sometimes high up on coastal cliffs, continues to flower. It begins

Coltsfoot (Tussilago farfara)

flowering in April, and by growing low and clinging tightly to precipitous rocky surfaces it goes on flowering into mid-autumn, in spite of the harsh environment.

November and December are difficult months for wild flowers. I chose the ivy (*Hedera helix*) with its pale yellow-green flowers for November, but I had to cheat a little for December. Quite understandably, few wild flowers venture to bloom in this month. Only flowers like shepherd's purse, groundsel and common chickweed seem to risk raising their heads at this time of year, and I didn't consider any of them very attractive, so I settled for some holly berries that are at least bright, cheerful and seasonal.

By January, some hardy plants are beginning to flower. The lovely alpine snowbell (*Soldanella alpina*) often flowers while the ground is still covered with snow. I would dearly love to grow some in my alpine house but, having kept a small plant for two years, watching it struggle to hang on to life and then finally die without a sign of a flower, I have come to the conclusion that, like all wild things, it needs to grow unshackled and free in the cold alpine conditions that are its natural habitat.

Finally, February is represented by the ubiquitous coltsfoot (*Tussilago farfara*). This is always the first wild flower to appear in our garden. Its bright cheery flowers respond to the weak sun of a mild February afternoon and assure us that spring is not far away.

I have kept the same wording for the explanation of how to use the almanack as appeared on Elizabeth Knowles' sampler. It seemed clear and concise. The dominical letter refers to the seven letters A to G denoting Sundays in any year. To take an example, the fiftieth anniversary of the D-Day Invasion occurred on Monday 6th June

1994. If we wanted to find out on which day the landings took place fifty years ago, first find the year 1944 under 'Years'. The dominical letter above this year is A. Find the month of June in the centre of the almanack and, with your finger, trace across to the right until you come to the letter A. Above this are the dates of all the Sundays of that month – 4th, 11th, 18th and 25th. The 6th June of that year was therefore a Tuesday – a fact confirmed by a commemorative reprint of my local paper for that day. You can have a lot of fun with this almanack, finding out on what day you were born, on what day your parents were married and so on.

I have had such a lot of enjoyment researching the mechanics behind Elizabeth Knowles' 18th-century almanack and devising an up-to-date equivalent. I hope that you will enjoy it too.

DANDELION CLOCK

As a partner for the almanack, and continuing the theme of time, I have designed a clock. The natural choice of wild flower for this was the common dandelion (*Taraxacum officinale*) whose lovely silky globe of seeds forms the familiar 'clock' of children's games. Love them or hate them, these cheerful flowers grow everywhere in early summer, and bring a touch of sunshine to grass verges throughout the land.

If you do not want to embark on a large project like an almanack or a clock, you will find that any one of these wild flower motifs will fit into a card for a special birthday. The flowers for each month from the almanack would be particularly appropriate for this purpose. You may wish to combine some of the motifs to make a picture or a decorative border along a table runner. The possibilities are endless.

Dandelion clocks
(Taraxacum officinale)

PERPETUAL ALMANACK

THE EMBROIDERY

Find the centre point on your piece of Aida
fabric, and the centre of the line below the
month 'May' on the chart. Begin working
in backstitch from this point. Use two
strands of cotton in the needle for all backstitch and cross stitch. You may prefer to
complete the grids and all the borders of
your almanack before working the numbers,
letters and flowers, etc. When working the
flowers, always work the cross stitch first
and add the backstitch to complete the
detail.

Steam press the finished embroidery
on the wrong side.

MOUNTING THE EMBROIDERY

Centre the fabric over the card for mounting. Fold the fabric over the card and lace it
across the back according to the instructions in Basic Techniques (see page 126).

Frame the almanack according to your
own preferences.

Key to Chart – Flower Panels

		DMC	Anchor	Madeira			DMC	Anchor	Madeira
⊥	Black	310	403	Black	●	Dark blue-green	500	879	1705
∷	Silver-grey	762	234	1804	✳	Dark green	3345	268	1406
•	White	Blanc	1	White	⊏	Deep green	3346	817	1407
⊞	Reddish-brown	221	897	0811	⊆	Green	3347	266	1408
▬	Dusky pink	223	894	0812	▽	Greenish-brown	3011	845	1607
╱	Light dusky pink	224	893	0813	⊔	Palest green	3348	265	1409
∟	Clear yellow	307	289	0104	⊡	Greenish-fawn	3013	842	1605
Z	Dull gold	725	305	0108	÷	Light fawn	3012	844	1606
╲	Bright yellow	973	290	0105	K	Pale green	472	264	1414
T	Navy	939	127	1009	◆	Brown	610	889	2106
▲	Purplish-blue	333	119	0903	◸	Gold	972	298	0107
✕	Blue	340	118	0902	⊠	Dull yellow	743	297	0113
⟍	Pale blue	341	117	0901	+	Golden brown	435	365	2010
⊢	Blue-green	501	878	1704	V	Cream	745	300	0111
○	Light blue-green	502	876	1703	⤬	Light gold-brown	436	363	2011
▼	Maroon	3685	70	0602	⅃	Deep purple	550	102	0714
▪▪	Dark red	815	43	0513	⊥	Purple	552	101	0713
⫽	Bright red	606	335	0209	△	Mauve	553	98	0712
⊔	Dull pink	351	10	0214	⅂	Pale mauve	554	96	0711
→	Dark pink	350	11	0213	⅁	Purplish-pink	3608	86	0709
←	Dull red	816	799	0511	⋉	Light pink	3609	85	0710
⊢	Red	817	46	0211	⏐	Pale pink	963	23	0608
⫽	Orange	740	316	0202					

Note Backstitch: *Title lettering* – capitals in maroon; and lower case letters in black. *Wood anemone* – flower centres, outline of flowers and bud in green; leaf stalk in deep green; and flower stems in dusky pink. *Greater butterwort* – flower stems in dusky pink. *Lords-and-ladies* – base of flower in brown. *Scarlet pimpernel* – flower stalks in palest green and calyxes in green. *Creeping bellflower* – flower stalks in deep green. *Evening primrose* – top edge of flower petals and bud in light gold-brown, edges of lower flower petals and bud (adjacent to area worked in 'gold' cross stitch) in golden brown, and the flower centre in deep green. *Heather* – stems in brown. *Thrift* – flower stalks in blue-green. *Ivy* – stems in brown and leaf veins in pale green. *Holly* – berry stalks in brown. *Alpine snowbell* – all stems and stalks in dusky pink; and calyxes of flowers and bud in light dusky pink.

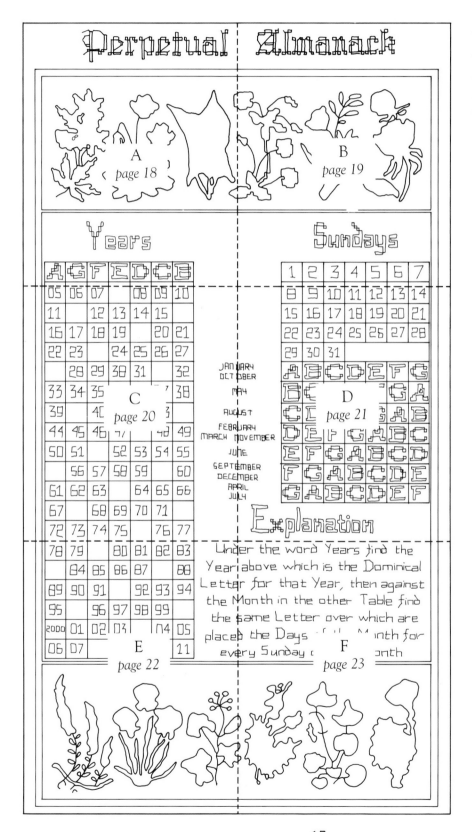

The chart for the perpetual almanack has been split over six pages. Refer to this diagram to check the relevant page on which each section of the chart falls.

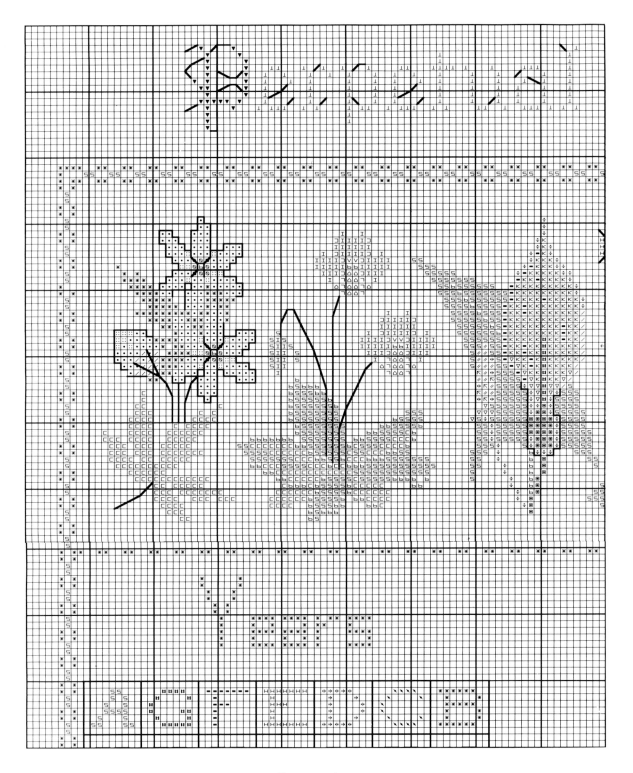

Section A

Section B

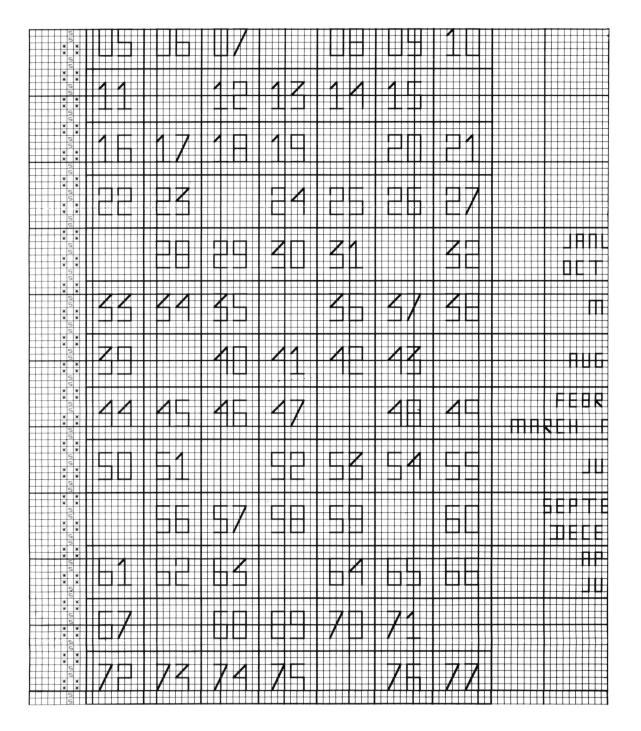

Section C

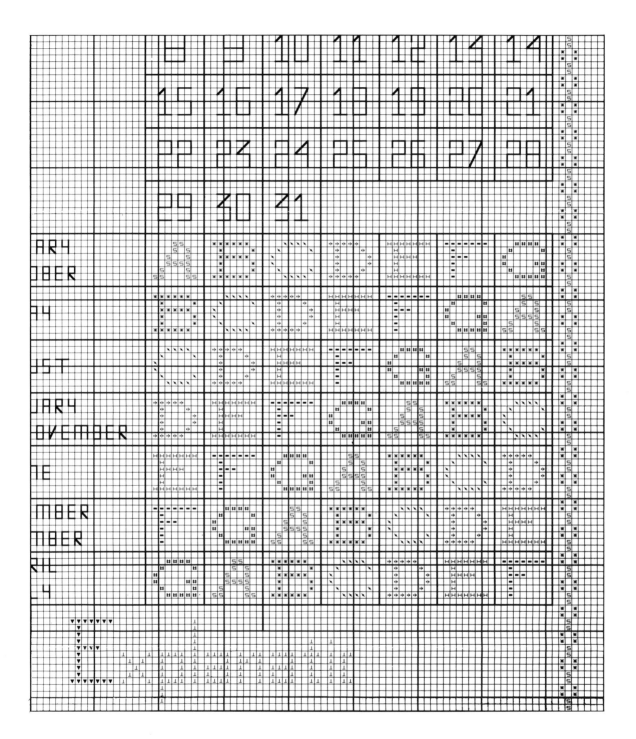

Section D

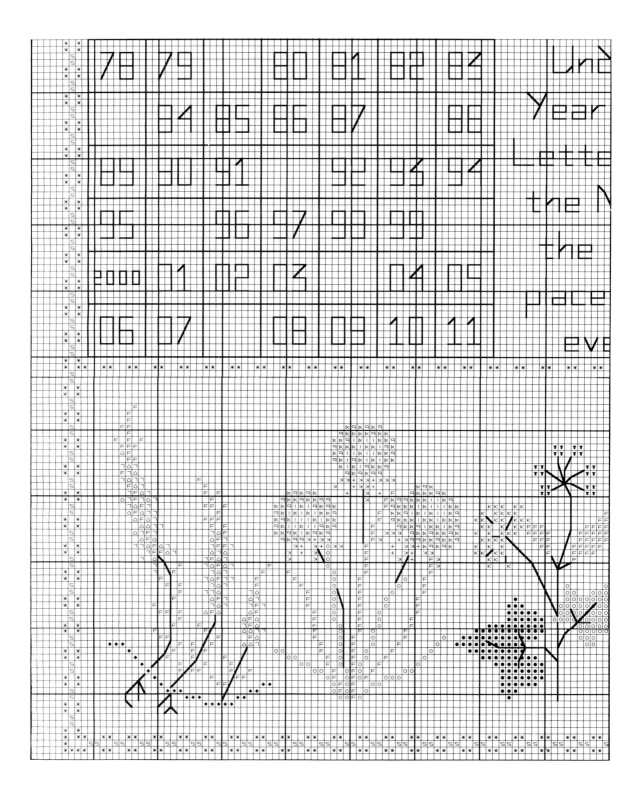

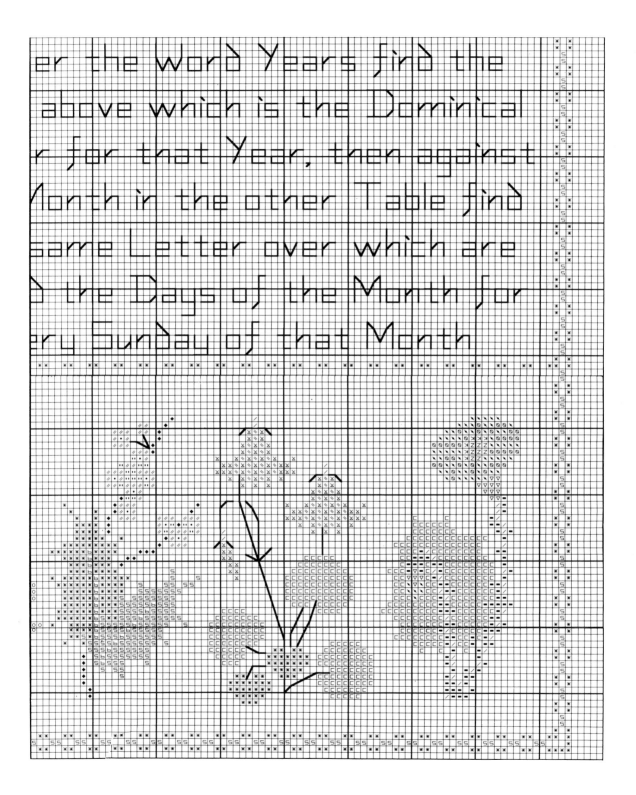

er the Word Years find the
above which is the Dominical
r for that Year, then against
Month in the other Table find
same Letter over which are
the Days of the Month for
ery Sunday of that Month

DANDELION CLOCK

YOU WILL NEED

The finished clock measures 20cm (8in) square.

- 30cm (12in) square of 18-count slate-grey Aida fabric
- No 26 tapestry needle
- Stranded embroidery cotton in the colours given in the panel
- 30cm (12in) of iron-on interfacing
- Perspex clock, see page 127 for suppliers

THE EMBROIDERY

Find the centre point on your piece of Aida fabric and on your chart. From this point, count down and across to find the nearest stitch of the dandelion seedhead to the centre, and begin at this point. For stitches incorporating a metallic thread, use one strand of blending filament with one of six-stranded cotton. For all other cross stitch and backstitch, use two strands of cotton.

When the embroidery is complete, steam press very carefully on the wrong side, using a cloth to prevent the iron from coming into direct contact with the metallic blending filament.

ASSEMBLING THE CLOCK

Back the finished embroidery with the iron-on interfacing. (NB: Do *not* attempt to cut your material to the final size until you have

KEY TO CHART – DANDELION CLOCK

		DMC	Anchor	Madeira
•	Silver metallic	Ecru	926	Ecru + Kreinik blending filament 001
Z	Dark yellow	725	305	0108
\	Yellow	973	290	0105
II	Lemon	726	295	0109
✳	Dark green	935	862	1505
5	Green	3346	817	1407
b	Pale green	3348	265	1409
	Light green *	3347	267	1408
⊘	Yellow-brown	831	888	2201
	Dark navy *	939	127	1009
	Dark grey & silver metallic *	413	401	1713 + Kreinik blending filament 001

NOTE Backstitch the numbers on the clock face in dark navy*; the lower petals of the dandelion flower in light green*; all dandelion seeds in dark grey and silver metallic*; and the centre of the dandelion flower in yellow-brown (*used for backstitch only).

done this.) Slide the finished design down between the two plates of clock perspex for a trial run. Measure carefully how much fabric you need to cut off the bottom of your embroidery to ensure that the spindle hole matches the centre of the embroidery. Once you have got this right, trim the embroidery to fit exactly the shape of the clock.

Using a sharp craft knife, cut out the hole for the clock spindle, then follow the manufacturer's instructions to fit the clock mechanism.

Dandelion (Taraxacum officinale)

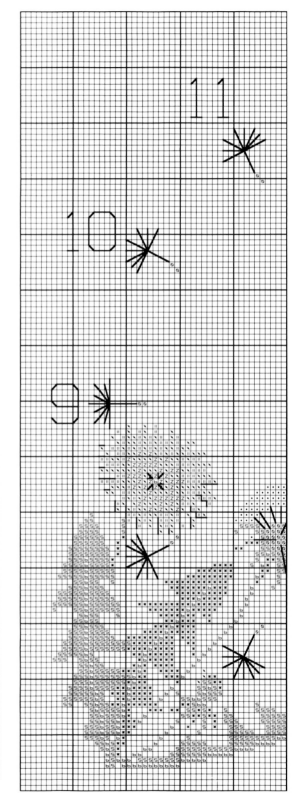

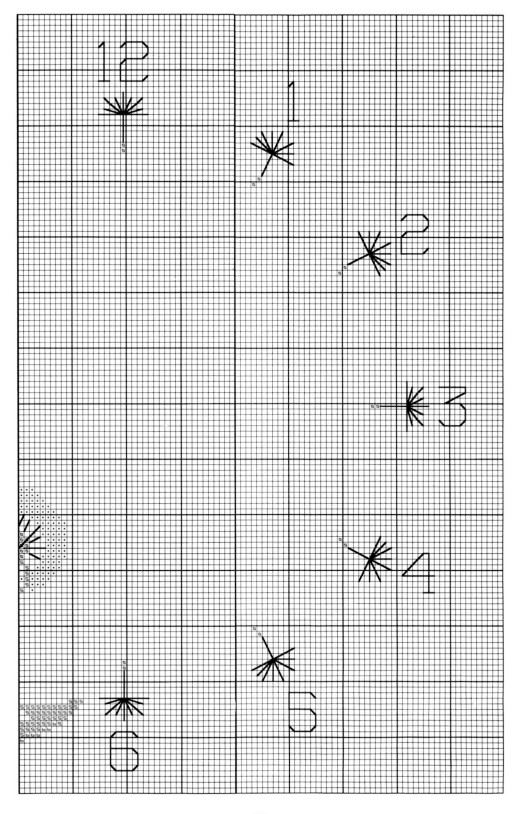

CHAPTER TWO

FIRESIDE COMFORT

WINNING COMPETITIONS is, sadly, not one of my fortes; however, a few years ago, to my surprise and delight, I learned that I had won a lovely greenhouse in a national gardening magazine competition. I decided that this little greenhouse, unlike our larger one at the bottom of the garden, should not become a repository for plant pots of all shapes and sizes, bulb bowls with last year's bulbs still in place, leaky old watering cans, half-used bottles of tomato feed and tangled heaps of wire, string and netting. This little greenhouse was to be used for something special. Thus began my interest in alpine plants.

I visited my local garden centre which specializes in the breeding of lewisias and I remember coming home with a shallow box packed tightly with pots of them in a striking range of colours – orange, apricot, deep rose, salmon pink, lemon and white. All lewisias originate from the western side of the USA, including the Rocky Mountains, and they flourish in a variety of habitats.

Lewisia tweedyi

The larger-flowered species, *Lewisia tweedyi*, with flowers 4cm (1½ in) across, are especially attractive, and I chose a delicate pink variety for the centre panel of my cushion.

ALPINE FLOWER DESIGN

My choice of alpines for the remaining eight panels was governed largely by their popularity and colour. For the top left-hand panel I chose the edelweiss (*Leontopodium alpinum*), native to the European Alps. It is familiar to any holiday-maker returning from Austria or Switzerland, and was popularized by the much-loved song of the same name from the film *The Sound of Music*. In its natural habitat it grows in inaccessible crevices high up in the Alps, but it can also be grown from seed. It will flourish in a garden border or rockery, providing the resident garden snails don't take a liking to it! The plant produces tufts of silvery-white leaves from which the flower stems sprout. Each stem produces star-like 'flowers' like miniature woolly starfish. The white woolly bracts surround and protect the tiny yellow flowers. It would be difficult to work a design of this plant on cream or white Aida because of its pale colours, but I found that it showed up well against the slate/rue green Aida fabric that I chose for this cushion.

Of all alpine flowers, the gentian must be the most evocative of the mountains. The spring gentian (*Gentiana verna*) is a true alpine flower, but it also grows in a few isolated areas of Britain, on the hillsides and mountains of the north, as well as in western Ireland. Its intensely blue flowers make it very much sought after by gardeners, and it has, therefore, suffered much at the hands of collectors. It is now a protected species in Britain.

Auricula (Primula auricula)

Yellow saxifrage (Saxifraga alpiculata)

The auricula (*Primula auricula*) is originally a native of the European Alps. Although the wild auricula has clear yellow flowers, the garden auriculas now come in a myriad colours. For this design I used my photographs of the very first auricula I ever bought. It was a particularly handsome specimen and it has inspired me to grow many more from seed since.

The windflower (*Anemone blanda*) is a delicate little flower originating from eastern Europe. Its daisy-like flowers, with soft petals often of a beautiful purplish-blue colour, are most attractive. I found the colour difficult to find in the range of six-stranded threads available. In painting you can always mix colours to acquire a suitable shade. With embroidery threads, the effect is more difficult to achieve. However, the windflower occurs in several colour variations so, hopefully, my choice of shades is acceptable to *Anemone blanda* enthusiasts!

The yellow saxifrage (*Saxifraga alpiculata*) with its sprays of primrose-coloured flowers and deep green foliage, provides a contrast to the other predominantly pinky-mauve and blue flowers. Just as it brightens the craggy crevices of its mountain home or our suburban rock gardens, it brings a spot of sunshine into my cushion design.

Continuing around the cushion in a clockwise direction, we come to lithodora heavenly blue (*Lithospermum diffusum*), a miniature shrub which spreads in prostrate fashion. It forms a wide mat of rather rough, dark-green foliage, and its 1cm (½ in) wide flowers are an intense gentian blue. I tried to grow it in my alpine house, but it much prefers my mother's garden wall, where it grows in profusion.

Pink saxifrage (Saxifraga 'Cranbourne')

The pink saxifrage (*Saxifraga* 'Cranbourne') grows in low symmetrical cushions. It has grey-green leaves and delightful rose-pink flowers. When I looked at my plant, flowering in the greenhouse last March, the short stamens glistened with a dewy substance. This prompted me to add a small amount of metallic thread to the stitches in the centre of the flower. If you do not wish to do this, it is not absolutely necessary, but I felt that it added something to the realism of the flowers.

Finally, the pasqueflower (*Pulsatilla vulgaris*) is now a rare plant in the wild, but it still grows on isolated areas of the chalky downlands of Britain. It flowers from spring to early summer and is a close relative of the colourful garden anemone. As well as its charming 'wide-eyed' flowers, it also has lovely feathery foliage which I thought would enhance the design.

AURICULA PICTURE

As a companion to the cushion, I have worked a picture which I have mounted in a round frame. Of the nine designs from the cushion, I chose the auricula, as it is a particular favourite of a friend of mine. My aim was to create an effect often achieved by watercolour artists and which I find particularly attractive. Detailed pencil sketches of botanical or other wildlife habitats have their main subject delicately highlighted in

Pasqueflower (Pulsatilla vulgaris)

watercolour. What I have tried to do here is to simulate this technique using embroidery threads, with the pencil lines replaced by dark grey backstitch, and the watercolour flower conveyed by the brighter colours of the cross stitch.

You could create your own picture of your favourite flower from the cushion design. The method I used is very simple. I made a copy of the auricula design, and extended the grid so that there were 20 free squares all the way around the flower. On the grid I then drew a simple pencil sketch of the Matterhorn and the surrounding Alpine peaks – the home of the original wild auricula. Then, following the pencil sketch lines as closely as possible, I marked in the route for my backstitch. Since backstitch can go across the lines of the grid diagonally, as well as horizontally and vertically, it is possible to follow the lines of the original sketch closely. I used the backstitch to outline the peaks, and also to represent the light and shade on the mountain slopes. Why not try your own picture? A lewisia against a backdrop of the Rocky Mountains, or a saxifrage against a background of craggy crevices would each make an original picture. Holiday photographs or travel brochures will supply you with some ideas.

VARYING THE DESIGNS

I worked my cushion design on 14-count Aida fabric, whereas the picture was done on 18-count material, which means that the work on the picture looks finer and the auricula flower smaller. You may like to work one of the alpine designs to mount in a card for a friend's birthday – or if you want a more permanent gift, mount the design in a small frame. You will need to decide how big you want your finished panel to be. The complete panels of the cushion, including the surround, are 76 squares by 76 squares. This means that on 14-count Aida, each panel will measure approximately 13.5cm (5½ in) square, on 18-count, 10.5cm (4¼ in) square and on 22-count, 9cm (3½ in) square.

You could work a combination of any number of panels on any count or any colour of evenweave fabric to make a picture for your wall, or you could extract just a single flower with a leaf or two to make into a mini-card or bookmark.

To create another gift for a gardener friend, you may like to work one of the alpine designs on a cover for a gardener's notebook. Follow the same instructions for making the recipe book cover (see page 83).

Worked over two threads on 28-count Linda, you could embroider half a dozen of these designs on place mats and matching serviettes. To finish these, simply machine stitch around the four sides of each article about 12mm (½ in) in from the edges, and remove the outer threads to form a fringe.

I am sure that you will think of many other uses for these designs, restricted only by your eyesight, your patience and by the fertility of your imagination.

ALPINE CUSHION

YOU WILL NEED

The finished cushion measures 49.5cm
(19½ in) square.

❧ Two pieces of 61cm (24in) square 14-count
slate/rue green Aida fabric
❧ No 24 tapestry needle
❧ Stranded embroidery cotton in the colours
given in the panel
❧ Two pieces of 61cm (24in) square strong
cotton material, to make the cushion pad
❧ 61cm (24in) cushion pad, or cushion filling
of your choice
❧ 2.4m (2¼ yd) braid

MAKING THE CUSHION

Take the two squares of cotton and, with
right sides together, and taking a 2.5cm
(1in) seam allowance, machine stitch
around the edges, leaving a 25cm (10in)
opening at one side. Trim across the corners
and turn right side out. Insert the pad or
filling and slipstitch the opening to close.

Place the embroidered piece of Aida
and the square of Aida which forms the
back, with right sides together, and repeat
as for the inner cover.

To complete the cover, trim the edges
with braid, mitring the corners neatly (see
page 125).

THE EMBROIDERY

Prepare the fabric by marking
the centre point with basting
stitches. Start to embroider
from the centre of the lewisia
panel. Use three strands of
cotton in the needle for the
cross stitch, and two strands
for the backstitch. For the
pink saxifrage, use one strand
of silver blending filament
with two strands of deep pink
for the stitches indicated in
the chart.

Steam press the finished
embroidery on the wrong side.

Windflower (Anemone blanda)

*K*ey to Chart – *A*lpine Cushion

		DMC	Anchor	Madeira			DMC	Anchor	Madeira
⊓	Dark grey	413	401	1713	⊡	Green	3346	817	1407
⊥	White	Blanc	1	White	÷	Pale green	3348	265	1409
∷	Yellow-green	472	264	1414	K	Pale blue-green	503	875	1702
•	Cream	746	275	0101	◆	Very light green	471	266	1501
▬	Pinkish-brown	223	894	0812	≡	Golden brown	833	874	2203
/	Grey-green	524	858	1511	⋉	Yellow brown	832	907	2202
∟	Bright lemon	727	293	0110	◗	Deep gold	725	305	0108
Z	Gold	743	297	0113	+	Dull green	3052	262	1509
⟍	Lemon	745	300	0111	V	Silvery-green	522	860	1513
‖	Pale yellow	744	301	0112	⋊	Light silvery-green	523	859	1512
T	Light navy	823	150	1008	⅃	Purple	550	102	0714
▼	Deep blue	797	132	0912	△	Mauve	209	109	0803
☐	Blue	798	131	0911	⌐	Pale mauve	210	108	0802
⟍	Light blue	322	978	1004	↑	Deep pink	3607	87	0708
▲	Purplish-blue	333	119	0903	⊐	Bright pink	3608	86	0709
△	Light purple	552	101	0713	⋈	Pink	3609	85	0710
⋈	Deep mauve	208	110	0804	I	Pale pink	3689	49	0607
◇	Wedgewood	340	118	0902		Light pinky-brown*	224	893	0813
⟍	Pale blue	800	129	0908		Khaki brown*	830	277	2114
И	Pale grey	318	399	1802		Ecru*	Ecru	926	Ecru
Χ	Light green-grey	3072	397	1805					
▼	Dark red	814	44	0514					
▪▪	Deep red	815	43	0513					
∥	Silver metallic	3607	87	0708 + Kreinik blending filament 001					
▽	Pinkish-mauve	553	98	0712					
—	Pale lilac	211	342	0801					
∗	Deep yellow	742	303	0107					
●	Dark blue-green	500	879	1705					
✳	Dark silver-green	520	862	1514					
⊏	Blue-green	501	878	1704					
⊐	Light blue-green	502	876	1703					
▽	Light green	3347	266	1408					
⊔	Greyish-green	927	849	1708					
■	Dark green	3345	268	1406					

NOTE Backstitch as follows: *edelweiss* – outer bracts in dark green and small yellow flowers in centre in dark grey; *auricula* – flower centre in ecru; *pasqueflower* – centre of flower and lower edge of centre in khaki brown, and petals in purple; *lewisia* – stamens in light green and edges of petals in deep pink; *windflower* – leaf stalks in light pinky-brown and lower edge of flower centres in purple; *pink saxifrage* – flower stalk in blue-green; *yellow saxifrage* – flower centres in dark green. Work french knots as follows: *pink saxifrage* – one french knot in centre of each flower in white; *lithodora heavenly blue* – five french knots around light navy centre of each flower in white.

A
page 38

B
page 39

C
page 40

D
page 41

The chart for the alpine cushion has been split over four pages. Refer to this diagram to check the relevant page on which each section of the chart falls.

Section A

Section B

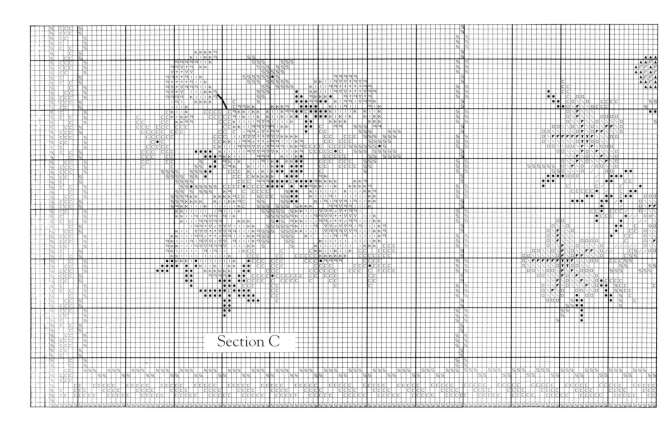

Section C

Spring gentian
(*Gentiana verna*)

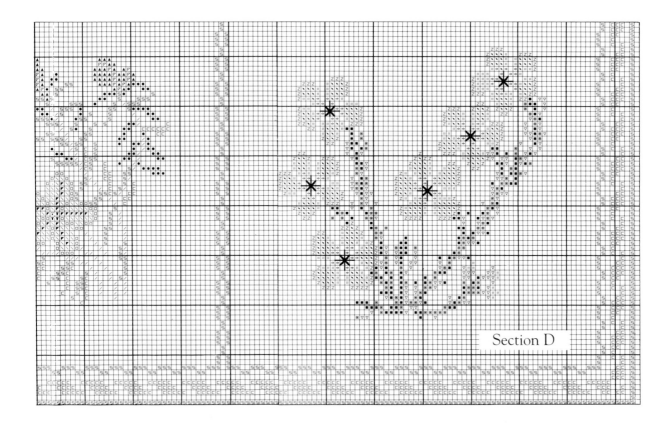

Section D

Circular Alpine Picture

You Will Need

The finished picture measures 15cm (6in) in diameter.

- 25cm (10in) square of 18-count cream Aida fabric
- No 26 tapestry needle
- Stranded embroidery cotton in the colours given in the panel
- 15cm (6in) diameter circular metal frame, see page 127 for suppliers

The embroidery

Find the centre point on your square of Aida fabric and, beginning from the centre of the chart, embroider the auricula, using two strands of cotton in the needle for both the cross stitch and the backstitch.

Steam press the finished embroidery on the wrong side.

Mounting the picture

Cut the piece of Aida to size, using the glass or acetate as a template. Mount according to the manufacturer's instructions.

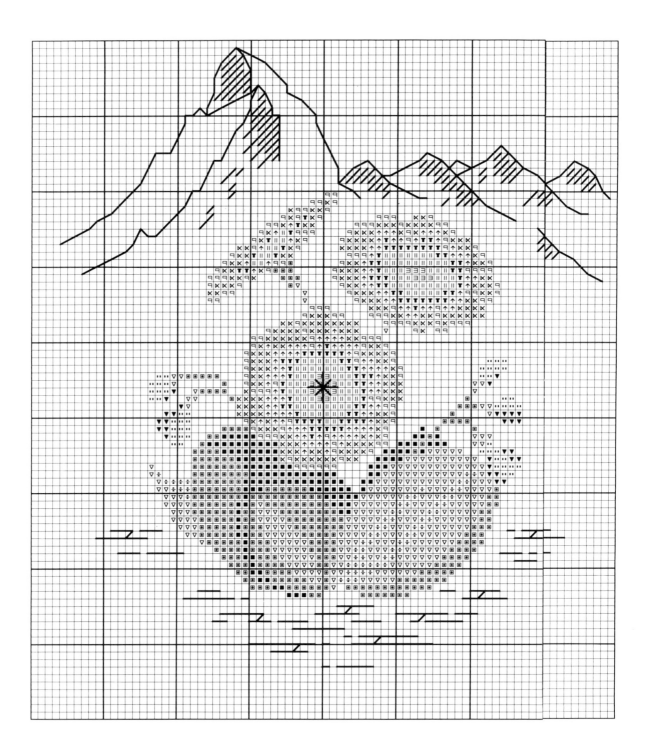

KEY TO CHART – CIRCULAR PICTURE (AURICULA)

		DMC	Anchor	Madeira
‖	Pale yellow	744	301	0112
⊤	Light navy	823	150	1008
▼	Dark red	814	44	0514
▪▪	Deep red	815	43	0513
▽	Light green	3347	266	1408
■	Dark green	3345	268	1406
⊡	Green	3346	817	1407
÷	Pale green	3348	265	1409
⊟	Golden brown	833	874	2203
↑	Deep pink	3607	87	0708
⊓	Bright pink	3608	86	0709
⋈	Pink	3609	85	0710
	Dark grey*	413	401	1713
	Ecru*	Ecru	926	Ecru

NOTE Backstitch the mountain background in dark grey* and the flower centre in ecru* (*used for backstitch only).

CHAPTER THREE

FLORAL HEIRLOOM

*T*F, LIKE ME, you enjoy visiting old houses, or browsing around stands at antique fairs, you cannot fail to have been impressed by the skill, care and craftsmanship that went into making some of the humblest of household articles in the past. As I look around the shops today, I wonder what, in a hundred years' time, will remain of our mass-produced goods, which are made to serve their purpose and are then thrown away. There are still good craftsmen around, but their work is swamped by the vast quantities of products, all identical and with no character or individuality of their own, which line the shelves of our stores. The pride, the love and the skill which went into creating a thing of beauty, seem almost to have disappeared. Even as a leisure activity, people protest that they haven't the time to make lovely things, yet I find it hard to believe they have less time than their grandparents who had none of the labour-saving gadgets we use today.

When I was drafting the outline for this book, I promised myself that at least one of the projects should be one which could be used by the embroiderer herself, and then passed on to her children or grandchildren. A needlework box was the perfect project. I thought the hexagonal shape was an unusual one, and it presented six side panels, as well as the lid, for cross stitch designs. To give the designs some unity, I decided on the theme of spring bulbs and corms.

SPRING BULB DESIGN

Of all the garden flowers, the spring bulbs are, I think, my favourites. From the rock-hard, snow-covered earth, these fragile flowers emerge with their fresh, bright colours and the promise of a new year ahead. In our front garden the first ones to emerge are the sunny yellow winter aconites peeping out from under last year's dead leaves. Species crocuses follow, each a colourful gem attracting the first bees and hoverflies of the season. Hard on their heels come the sky-blue scillas, the deep blue and purple *Iris reticulata*, the golden heads of the

Daffodils (Narcissus *sp.*)

Crocus *sp.*

Iris (Iris reticulata)

miniature daffodils and the diminutive pink cyclamen. These are the six flowers I chose for the side panels of the box, while the ivy circle provided a suitable design for the lid because, in our garden, ivy climbs around all the trees and hedges which form a back-drop for our spring bulbs.

Each of the six flower designs could be worked and mounted individually in a card. Alternatively, they could be made into a series of small pictures, or grouped to make a larger panel. The ivy design could be used to decorate a small mat for a dressing table.

As a companion to the workbox, I have included a needlecase. I chose the cyclamen design for this. From the original pattern I produced a mirror-image, and placed it 'back-to-back' with the workbox panel chart. If you prefer any of the other five designs, you can produce a mirror image of them by placing a copy of the chart face-down against a window and placing a piece of plain paper on top. You can trace the grid and chart, and then cut out the mirror image tracing and paste it in position back-to-back with the original design. Such a motif could be used as an edging for a table runner, a hand towel or a shelf.

*W*ORKBOX

THE EMBROIDERY

From the Aida fabric, cut out six pieces
measuring 15.5cm x 19cm (6in x 7½in) for
the six side panels, two pieces measuring
26.5cm (10½in) square to cover the top and
the base of the workbox, and six pieces
measuring 15.5cm x 6cm (6⅛in x 2⅜in) to
cover the six side pieces of the lid. Cut out
the same number and size of pieces from the
water silk. For each of the six side panels,
find the centre point on your piece of Aida
fabric and, beginning from the centre of the
chart, embroider one of the spring flower
designs, using two strands of cotton in the
needle for both the cross stitch and the
backstitch.

On the square to cover the top of the
workbox, find the centre of the ivy chart
and count carefully the number of squares
to the nearest dark blue-green ivy leaf.
Begin your stitching here, using two strands
of cotton in the needle for both the cross
stitch and the backstitch.

On the pieces for the sides of the lid,
work a rectangle 9 stitches by 53 stitches in
green, to match the panel borders.

Steam press on the wrong side of each
completed piece.

Iris (Iris reticulata)

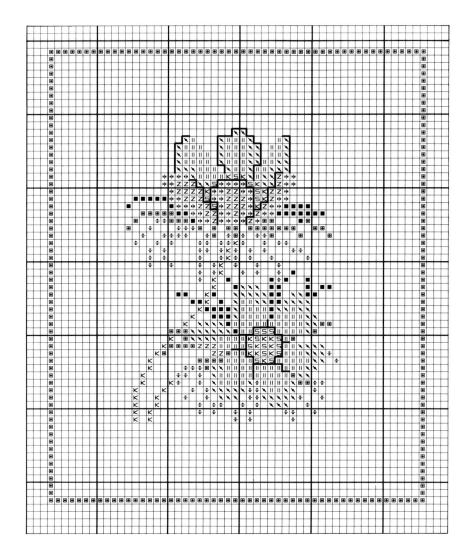

Key to Chart – Aconite

		DMC	Anchor	Madeira
Z	Light orange	743	297	0113
❭	Yellow	973	290	0105
‖	Lemon	307	289	0104
✛	Orange	972	298	0107
S	Yellow-green	471	266	1501
■	Dark green	3345	268	1406
☉	Green	3346	817	1407
÷	Light green	3347	266	1408

		DMC	Anchor	Madeira
K	Pale green	472	264	1414
	Light brown*	436	363	2011
	Brown*	435	365	2010

NOTE Backstitch the lines separating the petals on the lower flower and the three highest petals of the upper flower in light brown*; and around the centre of the lower flower and the lower petals of the upper flower in brown* (*used for backstitch only).

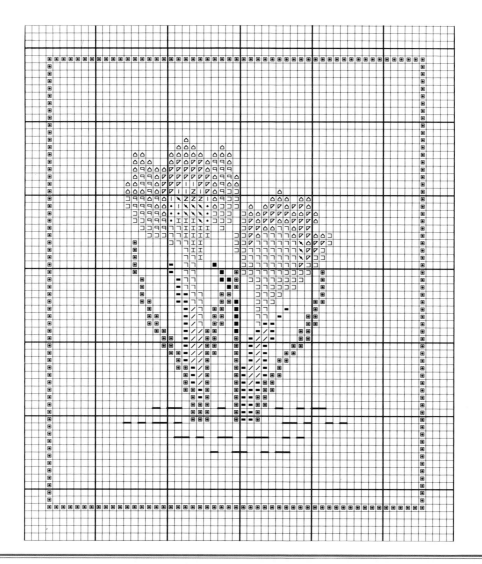

𝒦EY TO CHART – 𝒞ROCUS

		DMC	Anchor	Madeira			DMC	Anchor	Madeira
•	Ecru	Ecru	926	Ecru	⊥	Mauve	208	110	0804
▬	Fawn	841	378	1911	△	Pinkish-mauve	554	96	0711
╱	Pale fawn	842	376	1910	⊓	Pale mauve	210	108	0802
Z	Orange	722	323	0307	⊐	Purplish-pink	3609	85	0710
↘	Yellow	725	305	0108	I	Very pale pink	225	892	0814
▽	Pink	3689	49	0607		Light brown*	612	832	2108
■	Dark green	3345	268	1406					
⊡	Green	3346	817	1407	NOTE Backstitch the shadow on the ground in				
⊐	Light purple	553	98	0712	light brown* (*used for backstitch only).				

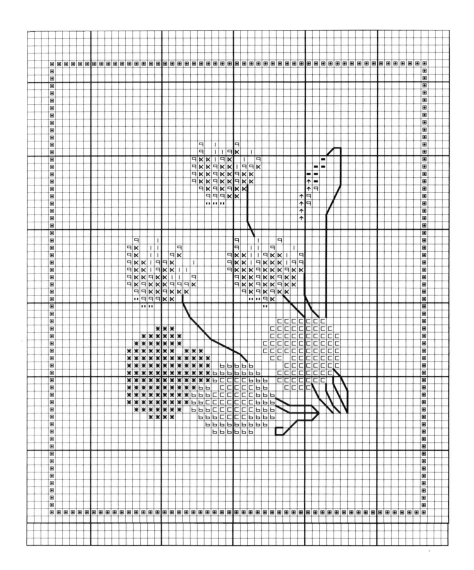

Key to Chart – Cyclamen

		DMC	Anchor	Madeira
▬	Reddish-brown	221	897	0811
▪▪	Dark red	814	44	0514
✳	Dark blue-green	500	879	1705
⊏	Blue-green	501	878	1704
┗	Mid blue-green	502	876	1703
⊡	Green	3346	817	1407
↑	Deep pink	3607	87	0708

		DMC	Anchor	Madeira
⊓	Pink	3608	86	0709
⋈	Light pink	3609	85	0710
❙	Very pale pink	225	892	0814
	Brownish-pink*	223	894	0812

Note Backstitch all stems in brownish-pink* (*used for backstitch only).

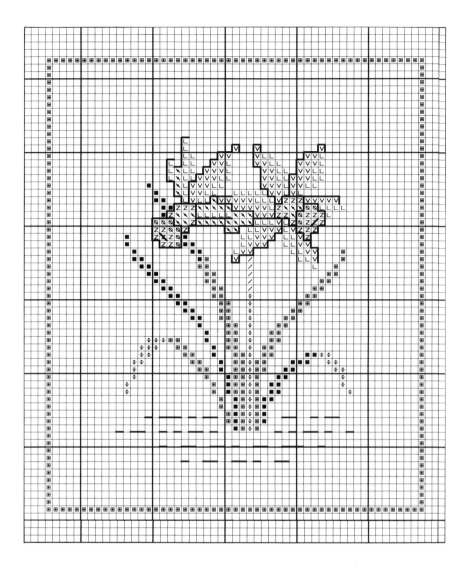

𝒦EY TO CHART – 𝒟AFFODIL

		DMC	Anchor	Madeira			DMC	Anchor	Madeira
/	Mushroom	841	378	1911	V	Lemon green	727	293	0110
L	Pale gold	3046	887	2206		Fawn*	612	832	2108
Z	Deep yellow	725	305	0108		Dark brown*	3031	905	2003
↘	Yellow	726	295	0109					
■	Dark green	3345	268	1406					
⊡	Green	3346	817	1407					
÷	Light green	3347	266	1408					
⊗	Yellow-brown	833	874	2203					

NOTE Backstitch the petals of the left-hand flower in green; the shadow on the ground in fawn*; the corollas of the daffodils in dark brown*; and the petals of the right-hand flower in light green (*used for backstitch only).

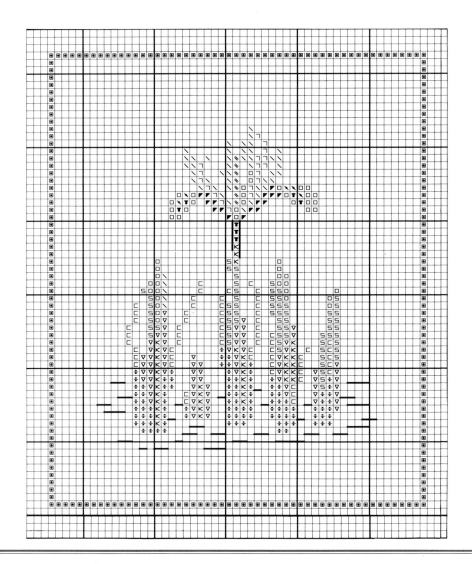

𝒦EY TO CHART – ℐRIS

		DMC	Anchor	Madeira			DMC	Anchor	Madeira
↘	Yellow	743	297	0113	▽	Pale green	3348	265	1409
T	Navy	939	127	1009	⊡	Green	3346	817	1407
◤	Navy + Deep	939+	127+	1009+	÷	Light blue-green	503	875	1702
	violet	333	119	0903	K	Light beige-green	644	830	1814
☐	Deep violet	333	119	0903	⌐	Lilac	210	108	0802
↘	Blue	340	118	0902		Light brown*	612	832	2108
↘	Pale blue	341	117	0901					
⊏	Blue-green	501	878	1704					
⊐	Mid green	3347	266	1408					

NOTE Backstitch the shadow on the ground in light brown* and the neck of the iris flower in navy (*used for backstitch only).

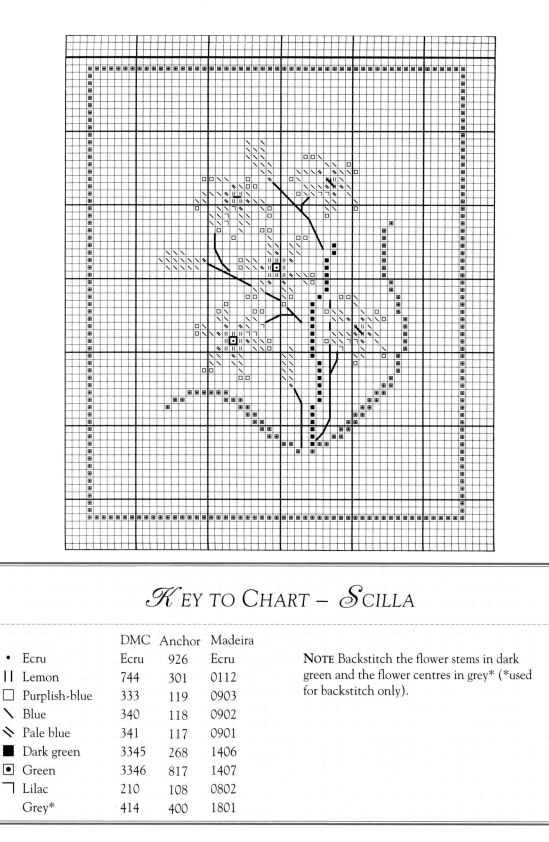

𝒦ey to Chart – 𝒮cilla

		DMC	Anchor	Madeira
•	Ecru	Ecru	926	Ecru
‖	Lemon	744	301	0112
☐	Purplish-blue	333	119	0903
╲	Blue	340	118	0902
╲	Pale blue	341	117	0901
■	Dark green	3345	268	1406
⊡	Green	3346	817	1407
⌐	Lilac	210	108	0802
	Grey*	414	400	1801

NOTE Backstitch the flower stems in dark green and the flower centres in grey* (*used for backstitch only).

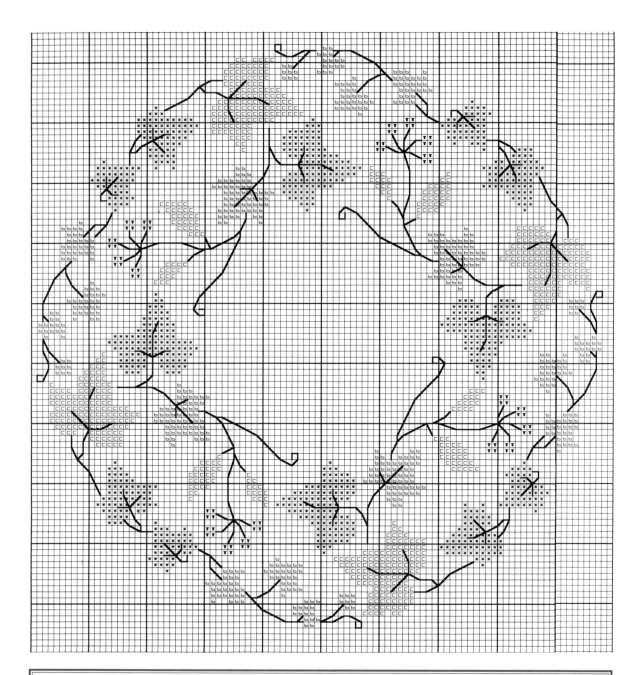

KEY TO CHART – IVY WREATH

		DMC	Anchor	Madeira
T	Dark navy	939	127	1009
✳	Dark blue-green	500	879	1705
⊏	Blue-green	501	878	1704
⊔	Mid blue-green	502	876	1703
	Greenish-brown*	610	889	2106
	Light green*	3348	265	1409

NOTE Backstitch the stalks and tendrils in greenish-brown* and the leaf veins in light green* (*used for backstitch only).

MAKING UP THE WORKBOX

Using the templates provided, cut the card to form the various parts of the box. Centre each design over the appropriate piece of card. Turn over the edges, and then lace across the back (see page 126).

From the lining material, make a narrow rouleau strip. To do this, cut a strip of lining material 111.5cm (44in) long and 2.5cm (1in) wide. Fold this in half lengthwise and machine stitch along the edge, taking a narrow turning. Turn the tube right side out and press. Then topstitch along both edges to produce a firm band.

Cut a piece of nylon wadding (batting) to the size of each section of the box. Place in position over the back of the laced embroidery and lay the lining over it. Turn in the edge and hem neatly.

Cut six pieces of rouleau each 15cm (6in) long – one for each of the side panels. Cut another piece of rouleau 20cm (8in) long for the base of the box.

To accommodate your selection of needlework tools, place the six rouleau strips across the lined side panels, and secure the ends, reserving the larger piece of rouleau for the base.

Now stitch all the six side panels to the base, making sure that flower panels of the same colours are not adjacent to one another. Assemble the lid of the workbox by stitching the six shallow side pieces to the hexagonal top and attaching the pieces to each other.

Attach a loop of elastic to alternate sides of the lid and a button to each corresponding panel of the base. To secure the lid to the workbox, simply fasten the elastic loops over the buttons on the base. Finally, place a button centrally on the top to facilitate the removal of the lid.

LID OF NEEDLEWORK BOX
CUT 1

SIDE OF NEEDLEWORK BOX LID
CUT 6

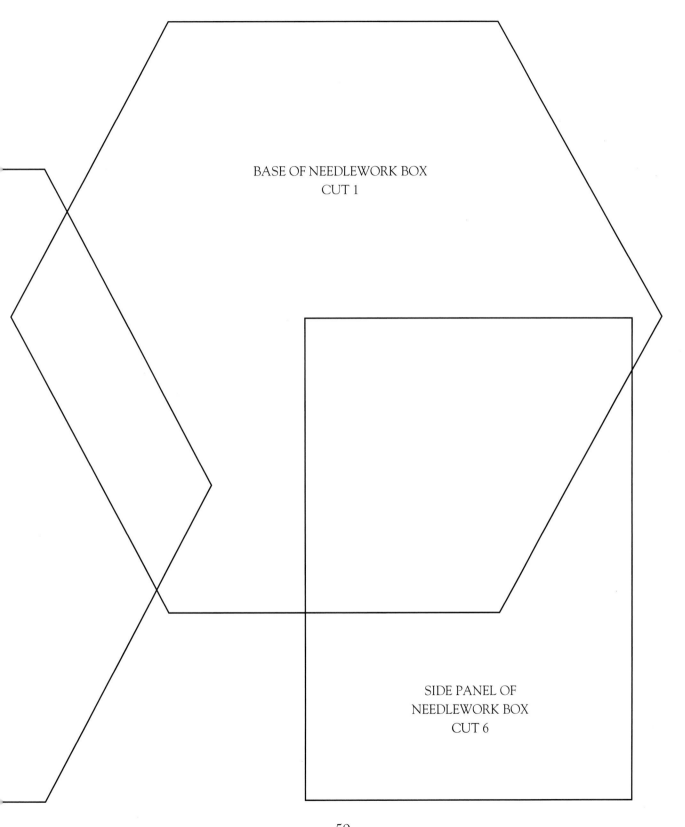

BASE OF NEEDLEWORK BOX
CUT 1

SIDE PANEL OF
NEEDLEWORK BOX
CUT 6

*N*EEDLEWORK CASE

*Y*OU WILL NEED

The finished needlework case measures
16cm x 10.5cm (6 ¼ in x 4¼ in).

- 42cm x 20cm (16½ in x 8in) of 18-count cream Aida fabric
- No 26 tapestry needle
- Stranded embroidery cotton in the colours given in the panel
- 31cm x 10.5cm (12 ¼ in x 4 ¼ in) of iron-on interfacing
- 35.5cm x 15cm (14in x 6in) of lining fabric
- 29cm x 9cm (11½ in x 3½ in) of felt
- 61cm (24in) of green ribbon, 6mm (¼ in) wide

THE EMBROIDERY

Fold the Aida fabric in two, producing a working surface measuring 21cm x 20cm (8¼in x 8in). With the fold on the left, measure 2.5cm (1in) in from the fold and mark a line from the top to the bottom of the Aida parallel with the fold. Find the centre point along this line, and the centre point along the left-hand border of the chart. Begin working from this point.

Use two strands of cotton in the needle for both the cross stitch and the backstitch.

Steam press the embroidery on the wrong side when complete.

MAKING THE NEEDLECASE

Trim the Aida to 37cm x 16cm (14½ in x 6¼ in). Make and press a 2cm (¼ in) turning on all sides, mitring the corners neatly (see page 125).

Slide the interfacing under the turnings and iron it in place. Turn under 12mm (½ in) all around the lining and hem it to the Aida to cover the interfacing.

Attach the felt to the inside of the case by lightly stitching it down the centre. Tie the ribbon into a bow and use it to trim the spine of the needlework case.

*K*EY TO CHART – *N*EEDLEWORK CASE

		DMC	Anchor	Madeira
▬	Reddish-brown	221	897	0811
❞	Dark red	814	44	0514
✳	Dark blue-green	500	879	1705
⊏	Blue-green	501	878	1704
┗	Mid blue-green	502	876	1703
⊡	Green	3346	817	1407
↑	Deep pink	3607	87	0708
⊣	Pink	3608	86	0709
⋈	Light pink	3609	85	0710
I	Very pale pink	225	892	0814
	Brownish-pink*	223	894	0812

NOTE Backstitch all stems in brownish-pink* (*used for backstitch only).

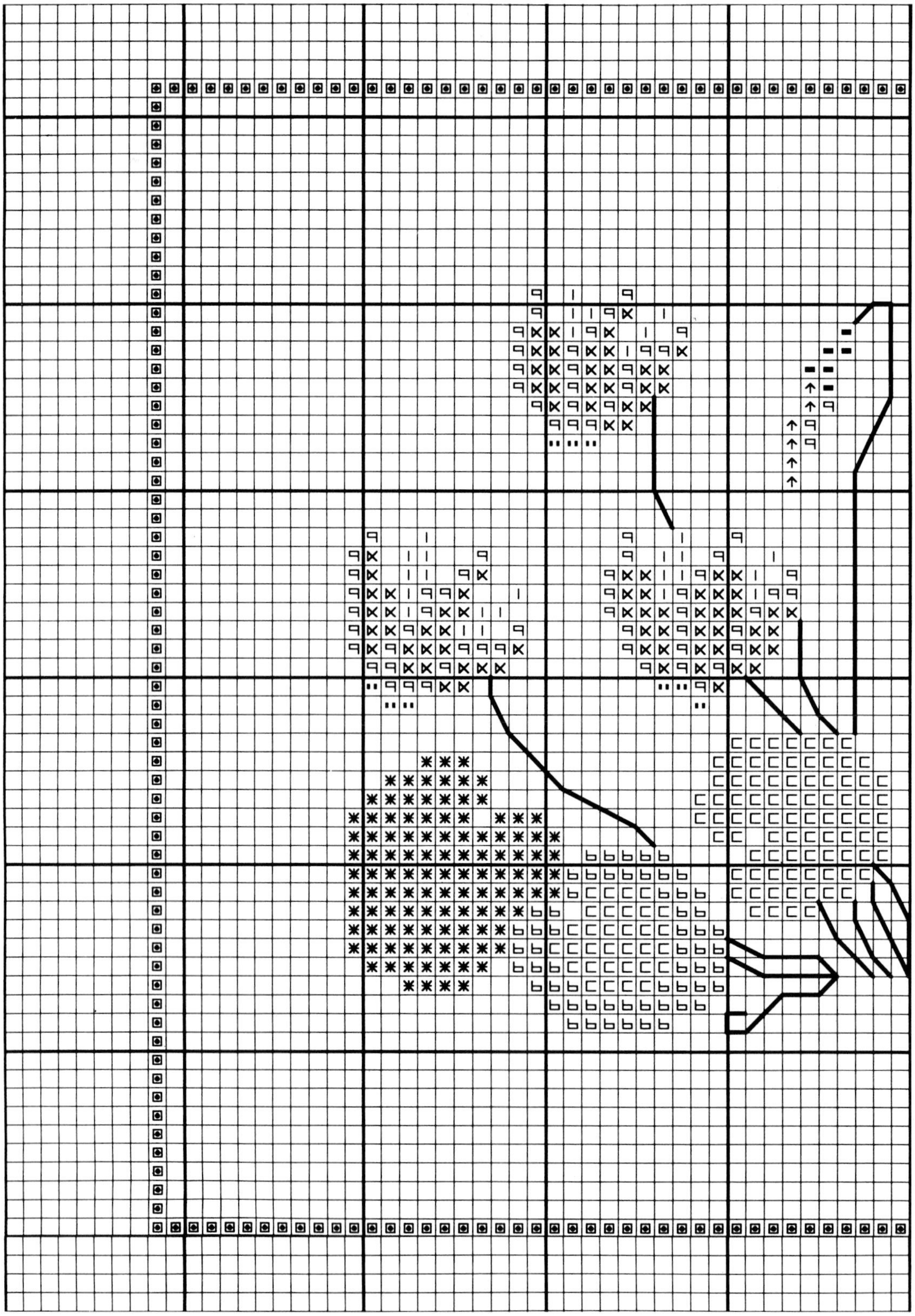

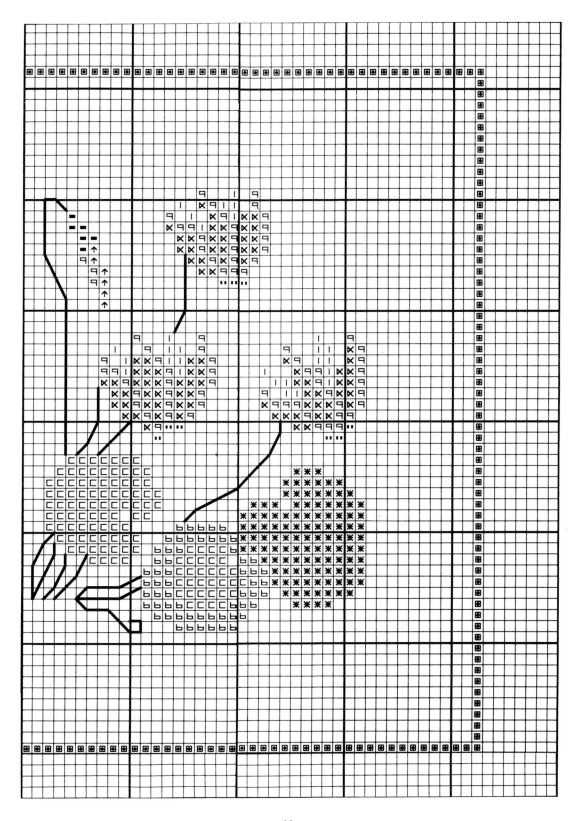

CHAPTER FOUR

AN ENGLISH COUNTRY GARDEN

THE CHARM of a typical cottage garden is in the impression it gives of natural, unplanned luxuriance, and in the perfume and colour of its flowers. The cottage garden developed in the 19th century, and was very different from the stylish, formal gardens of the larger houses, which had dominated garden design for centuries. A typical country cottage garden would have low-growing shrubs like lavender along the path, where clothing, brushing against them, would release a lovely perfume. Clove-scented pinks would also be favourites, planted along paths, near doors and under windows. Further back in the border would be lupins, irises, aquilegias, foxgloves and lilies, with roses and honeysuckle around the cottage door. Standing in stately fashion against walls and buildings would be the delphiniums and hollyhocks. My problem was to design a composite picture of cottage flowers, but at the same time stitch them in such a way that they were recognizable plants, rather than just a random mass of coloured blobs. I hope that I have conveyed something of the random planting in such a garden, without losing the identity of the individual flowers.

Delphinium (hybrid)

COTTAGE GARDEN

The tall, stately hollyhock has been a favourite in country gardens for centuries. The traditional single variety has changed little over the years. The ones shown in engravings, in 16th- and 17th-century books of herbs, look identical to the ones seen growing in gardens today. The tall hollyhock (*Alcea rosea*) is a member of the mallow family. Its long swaying stems bear large flowers, which open from the bottom of the stem right to the top. Hollyhocks

come in shades of pink, dark crimson, red, maroon, yellow and white. I remember well these towering flower stems growing along the side wall of my grandparents' garden. My grandmother was crippled with arthritis, and was unable to move from her chair. She spent her days sitting in her small living room, looking down her narrow back garden. Little else grew in the garden, but I remember that the beautiful colours of the hollyhock flowers gave her a lot of pleasure in the summer. I was cheered to find some fine specimens of old-fashioned hollyhocks growing in the station garden at Llangollen, in Wales, this summer, and it is from photographs I took there that I was able to design this flower stem.

No cottage garden is complete without the tall spikes of delphinium flowers. They grow beautifully in my aunt Lilian's garden, where, in summer she has lavender, deep blue and purple, single and double varieties. They form a dramatic backdrop to her pretty flower borders. Sadly, in our garden, which tends to be very damp, any young delphinium plants quickly become a tasty meal for the snails and slugs. I was amazed to discover that delphiniums are produced by hybridization from the wild Eurasian species *Delphinium elatum*, and that this, in its turn, is a member of the buttercup family. Maybe, using your imagination, you can detect the relationship in the leaves!

LUPINS, PINKS & LAVENDER

Lupins, too, are inseparable from the image of a traditional cottage garden, although these colourful and popular hybrids are a product of only the last 100 years; and it was only in the 1930s that George Russell grew many of the earlier lupins from seed. With great patience and meticulous selection, he created the much-loved Russell strain. The flowers come in a great range of blues, pinks and yellows, and many of the spectacular spikes are bicoloured. I had to include a lupin in my picture because it was one of the first flowers that I learned to recognize in the garden of my childhood home in Birmingham. They grew in enormous, vigorous clumps, and in a lovely blend of colours. The leaves of the lupin always fascinated me. They are shaped like many-fingered hands, and in the umbilical depression, where all the leaflets meet, droplets of water collect after a shower of rain. These water droplets shine in a myriad of rainbow colours when the sun shines on them. I was tempted to stick one of my tiny diamante stones right in the centre of the leaf to produce this effect, but then I thought that

such an addition may not be to everyone's taste, so I will just leave this idea with you.

The old-fashioned pinks also belong in a typical country garden. On a hot, summer day, their flowers fill the air with the rich, sweet scent of cloves. These plants are often used to bring colour to the front of an herbaceous border, hiding the stems of the taller plants behind, which can sometimes look a little unsightly. Their colours range from white, through pinks, to deep crimson. I have chosen a deep pink one here, to blend with the maroon-red of the hollyhock and the pinks of the lupin.

To complete the country garden picture, I have added a plant of old-fashioned lavender. The popularity of lavender goes back many centuries. The Greeks and Romans loved its fresh, clean perfume, and used it in their bath-water. Its name comes from the Latin *lavare* meaning 'to wash'. Lavender was strewn on the floors of houses to mask unpleasant smells, and also to act as an insect repellent. It was valued for its insect-repelling properties just as much then as it is by those walking in damp woodlands on a summer evening today. In the past, lavender has been used to ward off plagues, and to cure headaches and dizziness, but nowadays its healing properties are acquired from essential oil, which is distilled from the flowers, leaves and stems. Our lavender bush, growing by the porch door, is a magnet for bees and hoverflies in the summer, while in the winter its silvery foliage gives shelter to ground-feeding birds like wrens, dunnocks and robins.

I hope you enjoy working this picture, but if you want to do a smaller project, you may extract a single plant to work on a greetings card, a lavender bag, or other small item.

*G*ARDEN *P*ICTURE

THE EMBROIDERY

Find the centre point on your piece of Aida fabric, and the centre point on the chart. Starting from this point, and using two strands of cotton in the needle, complete the cross stitch. Then work the backstitch, also using two strands of cotton. Steam press on the wrong side when finished.

MOUNTING & FRAMING

Centre your embroidered picture over the cardboard, ensuring that the lines of the threads run parallel with the edges of the card. Lace the embroidery over the mount (see page 126) in a frame of your choice.

*Delphinium
(Delphinium elatum)*

*K*EY TO CHART – *G*ARDEN PICTURE

		DMC	Anchor	Madeira
∷	Ecru	Ecru	926	Ecru
⊞	Dull maroon	902	897	0601
╱	Cream	677	886	2207
∟	Lemon	727	293	0110
╲	Yellow	444	291	0105
‖	Light grey-green	3013	842	1605
T	Light navy	336	816	1006
◢	Purplish-blue	333	119	0903
◻	Blue	799	130	0910
╲	Lavender blue	340	118	0902
◇	Light blue	800	129	1002
╲	Pale blue	341	117	0901
⊏	Yellow-green	3346	817	1407
▼	Light maroon	814	44	0514
▪▪	Dark red	816	799	0512
⫽	Dull pink	3350	42	0603
⊔	Deep pink	602	63	0702
▽	Pink	603	62	0701
—	Pale pink	605	60	0613
⊹	Dark pink	335	41	0506
●	Very dark green	934	862	1506
✳	Dull green	3362	861	1601

		DMC	Anchor	Madeira
⊏	Dark green	937	268	1504
⊐	Green	3363	262	1602
⊔	Pale green	472	264	1414
■	Dark blue-green	500	879	1705
⊡	Blue-green	501	878	1704
÷	Light blue-green	502	876	1703
K	Pale blue-green	503	875	1702
V	Light green	3347	266	1408
⋊	Greyish-green	3364	260	1603
	Grey*	413	401	1713

NOTE Backstitch the leaf veins of the delphinium leaf in greyish-green; the centres of the holly-hock flowers in grey*; the leaf veins of all holly-hock leaves, except the darkest leaf, in pale blue-green; all lavender stalks, and the stalks of the small upper leaves of the hollyhock in green; the leaf vein of the darkest hollyhock leaf in light blue-green; the flower and leaf stalks of the delphinium in light green; and the centres of the pinks in dark blue-green (*used for back-stitch only).

CHAPTER FIVE

COOK'S HERBAL DELIGHTS

FROM TIME IMMEMORIAL, plants have provided man with healthy, tasty foods. Herbs have helped to cure man's ailments and heal his wounds; they have served to provide him with cosmetic preparations, with delicate, natural perfumes and with safe disinfectants; they have provided him with subtle shades of natural colour with which to dye wool, silk, unbleached cotton and linen, and they have given him preparations to embalm the bodies of the dead.

HISTORY OF HERBS

Herbs, in early days, embraced any plant which was useful to man. It was the Romans, 2,000 years ago, who introduced 200 different herbs into Britain. Many of them, like sage, borage and thyme, are very familiar to us today. During the 400 years of occupation, many of these herbs became naturalized and now grow wild.

With the establishment of the Christian church many great monasteries were founded, and the herbs left by the Romans were cultivated by the monks as the raw materials for medicines and healing balms. Through the Middle Ages, the use of herbs in the home grew steadily and all sorts of myths and folklore grew up around them and were passed on from generation to generation.

In the 16th century, the first scientific studies of plants in Britain were made, and the cultivation of herbs continued to flourish through to the 19th century. In the 20th century, however, the growth of scientific knowledge made it possible to isolate chemical substances from plants and to synthesize their properties. An accurate dosage of drugs could be prescribed and administered, and they could be purchased quite easily at the local chemist. Modern methods of manufacturing made it possible to produce synthetic flavourings in bottles, additives to colour and preserve food, and synthetic dyes for textiles. The traditional herb industry faltered and finally disappeared, but in the countryside, and especially in Mediterranean countries, herbal knowledge has lived on.

During the last couple of decades, we have all become aware of the dangerous side-effects resulting from the use of preservatives in food and the addition of artificial agents to enhance colour and flavour. We have also become aware of the loss of natural flavour as a result of the decline in the use of natural herbs in the preparation of foodstuffs. Much has recently been written on the skills of cooking with herbs, and many cookery programmes on television have been devoted to herbs and the culinary arts. There has also been a resurgence in the use of natural herbs in cosmetics and the treatment of minor ailments, while craftsmen have sought to revive natural dyes to colour their threads and fabrics.

HERBAL DESIGN

For my design, I have chosen five common herbs, which I hope will be familiar to you all. The first plant is chives (*Allium schoenoprasum*), a hardy, perennial plant, with narrow, hollow leaves and lovely mauve-pink flowers. We grow it in our garden and it forms a pretty edging to the path through our vegetable plot. Its mild onion flavour makes it a valuable herb in the kitchen, where it is used as a garnish on many dishes including soup, eggs, fish and chicken, and also in salads and with vegetables. It is also included as a flavouring in cream cheese.

Chives (Allium schoeno-prasum)

The leaves are said to stimulate the appetite and promote digestion. They contain some iron and vitamins. The attractive flowers can be broken into individual florets and sprinkled on salads. Chives are useful to the gardener as the plants deter aphids, apple scab and mildew. Alternatively, the leaves can be used to make an infusion for spraying on other plants to protect them from such infestations.

For my second herb I chose borage (*Borago officinalis*), which grows semi-wild in our vegetable garden. It is a tall annual, with large, floppy, hairy leaves, but it is its clusters of pure blue, star-shaped flowers with dark centres which make it so attractive. The Celtic name *borrach* means 'courage', and the lovely flowers are sometimes floated in stirrup cups, where they are reputed to make the huntsmen more courageous. The flowers can also be used to garnish salads and sandwiches. Frozen into ice-cubes they look very decorative in drinks, and candied or crystallized they make delightful edible decorations on cakes or ice creams. Though the flowers are most definitely the most attractive part of the plant, the leaves are also useful. These can be chopped up in salads, in egg dishes, in salad dressing or with cucumber. Also an infusion can be made from the leaves which is believed to be a good tonic for reducing fevers and relieving liver and kidney complaints. In addition to its culinary and medicinal uses, the fresh, young leaves can be used to create a face pack for dry skin, and the flowers can be dried to give colour to pot pourri.

Comfrey (*Symphytum officinale*) is a tall, spreading perennial with coarse leaves and mauve or creamy-white flowers. The plant contains an impressive list of beneficial substances in its leaves. Fresh comfrey leaves laid on cuts and bruises are said to promote healing. The roots and leaves can be used to make a poultice or soothing ointment. From the root, a drink can be produced to help coughs and bronchial ailments. In the kitchen, the fresh young leaves can be chopped up in salads, cooked like spinach, or dipped in batter and eaten as fritters. The stems can be blanched and cooked like asparagus. For the gardener, comfrey is a good composting plant, helping rapid breakdown within the compost heap. Comfrey leaves can be soaked in water for four weeks to make a very effective tomato or potato fertilizer.

Tansy (*Tanacetum vulgare*) is an attractive and vigorous plant, with a round, ridged stem and indented, aromatic leaves. It bears dense, flat clusters of mustard-yellow flowers. Tansy is believed to have properties useful in arresting decay, and preserving the dead. According to classical legend, a drink made from tansy was given to the handsome Ganymede to make him immortal so that he could serve as Zeus's cup bearer. Appropriately, the flowers dry beautifully as 'everlasting flowers'. Medicinally, an infusion can be made from leaves and flowers to treat bruising, rheumatism and sprains, though it is said to irritate some skins. In the kitchen, leaves can be stewed with rhubarb or can be rubbed on meat to flavour it. Leaves hung indoors deter flies, while both leaves and flowers can be used to produce yellowish-green and golden yellow dyes.

Finally, I have included the attractive herb sage (*Salvia officinalis*), an aromatic evergreen shrub, popular with bees. It has narrow, coarse-textured leaves and soft, purple flowers. The sage plant has been praised for its power of promoting longevity. The name 'salvia' from the Latin *salvere*, meaning 'to be healthy' or 'to cure' reflects its reputation. An infusion made from its leaves and drunk hot is said to soothe coughs and colds, aid digestion and relieve constipation. Sage tea and sage wine are blood tonics. They freshen the mouth and

ease rheumatic pain. To the cook, sage is invaluable. As well as being an essential ingredient of sage and onion stuffing, the leaves can be used to flavour pâtés, sauces and dressings. Leaves are also cooked with fatty or strong-flavoured meats like pork, duck and game. In the home, dried leaves can be put among linen to discourage insects, while leaves boiled in water produce an effective disinfectant. Sage leaves can also be used to make an astringent cleansing lotion, and as a rinse to condition and darken grey hair. Rubbed on teeth, it will whiten them, and as a mouthwash it will freshen breath.

Using Herbs Today

In this latter part of the 20th century when, in so many ways man has become so sophisticated, it is reassuring to learn that he has not severed his ties with the natural world entirely. It is comforting to know that people are responding to the warning signs confronting them every day concerning the dangers of over-prescription of synthetic drugs and their side effects, synthetic chemicals in agricultural sprays and fertilizers, food additives and colourings, and are turning to more natural products. As well as being more healthy than their synthetic counterparts, herbs are also delightful plants in their own right. Whatever your special interest, whether in medicine, in beauty products, in gardening or in craft work, herbs have some valuable properties to contribute to your work; but it is, surely to the cook that herbs mean most of all. This design incorporating five of my favourite herbs is especially for the keen cook. I hope it will bring some of the fragrance and colour of the herb garden into your kitchen.

Kitchen Memo Board

You Will Need

The finished memo board measures 57cm x 37cm (22½in x 14½in).

- 81cm x 56cm (32in x 22in) of 14-count cream Aida fabric
- No 24 tapestry needle
- Stranded embroidery cotton in the colours given in the panel
- 57cm x 37cm (22½in x 14½in) of pinboard
- Strong thread, for lacing the embroidery over the pinboard

THE EMBROIDERY

Begin by working the border. Place your piece of Aida fabric on a table with one of the short sides along the bottom. Run a line of basting stitches across 13.5cm (5⅜in)

from the bottom edge of the material. Find the centre point along this line and begin working from the centre point of the lower border on the chart.

Use three strands of cotton in the needle for the cross stitch and two strands for the backstitch.

Steam press on the wrong side when complete.

MOUNTING THE EMBROIDERY

Find the centre of the board and the centre of the Aida fabric, and position the embroidery over the pinboard. Turn all the edges over and fold neatly at the corners. Lace the embroidery across the back according to the instructions on page 126.

You may wish to back your memo board with fabric or card, or you may prefer to leave it unbacked, as here, in order to facilitate washing from time to time.

Borage (Borago officinalis)

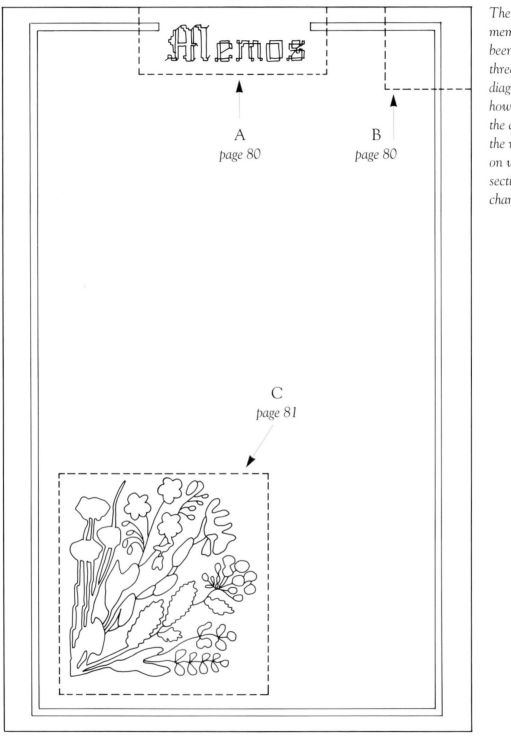

A
page 80

B
page 80

C
page 81

The chart for the memo board has been split into three. Refer to this diagram to check how to build up the chart and find the relevant page on which each section of the chart falls.

𝒦EY TO CHART –
𝒦ITCHEN MEMO BOARD & RECIPE BOOK COVER

		DMC	Anchor	Madeira
⊥	Black	310	403	Black
•	White	Blanc	1	White
Z	Dark yellow	725	305	0108
⟍	Yellow	726	295	0109
‖	Very light green	3013	842	1605
T	Navy	939	127	1009
⊦	Blue-green	501	878	1704
○	Light blue-green	502	876	1703
И	Pale blue-green	503	875	1702
↓	Dark blue	798	131	0911
∧	Blue	799	130	0910
▼	Maroon	902	897	0601
✳	Dark green	3345	268	1406
⊏	Deep green	3346	817	1407
⊐	Green	3347	265	1408
▽	Lime green	470	267	1502
⊔	Light lime green	471	254	1501
■	Leaf green	987	244	1403
⊡	Bright green	988	243	1402

		DMC	Anchor	Madeira
÷	Light green	989	242	1401
+	Dull green	3011	845	1607
V	Light dull green	3012	844	1606
⅄	Pale green	3348	264	1409
⊥	Dusky pink	316	969	0809
△	Light dusky pink	778	49	0808
⊓	Rose pink	776	24	0503
↑	Deep pink	3607	87	0708
⊐	Purplish-pink	3608	86	0709
⋉	Pink	3609	85	0710

NOTE Backstitch capital M of 'Memos' and the bases of the chive flower heads in deep pink; the flowers of the chives in purplish-pink; the tansy and borage stems in deep green; the sage and comfrey stalks in dull green; the stalk of the smallest tansy leaf in dark green; the calyxes of the borage flowers in green; the centres of the borage flowers in navy; the leaf veins of the comfrey in pale green; and the lower case letters of 'Memos' in black.

Repeating border –
Section B

Section A

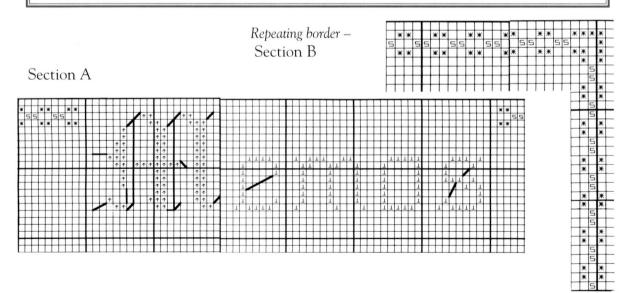

Section C

This chart can be used for both the memo board and the recipe book cover. To complete the memo board, refer to the diagram on page 78 and the charts on page 80.

Recipe Book

THE EMBROIDERY

Fold the piece of Aida fabric in half to give you a working surface of 28cm x 25cm (11in x 10in). Run a line of basting stitches along the fold. Measure in 2cm (¾in) to the right of this line and run a parallel line of basting stitches from the top to the bottom of the Aida. From the bottom of the Aida measure up 5cm (2in) and run a line of basting stitches through this point, parallel with the bottom edge. The point where these last two lines of basting stitches intersect is the bottom left-hand corner of the herb chart.

Beginning at this point, and using two strands of cotton in the needle, complete all the cross stitch first. Then work the backstitch, also using two strands of cotton in the needle.

Steam press on the wrong side when complete.

COVERING THE BOOK

Centre the iron-on interfacing lengthwise on the Aida fabric and press. Fold the Aida to form a narrow hem along all the edges, enclosing the interfacing. Machine stitch into position.

Centre the recipe book on the wrong side of the fabric. Fold the extra width over the front and over the back covers. Seam along the edges at the top and the bottom to form a pocket at the front and the back. Use the covered notebook to record all your favourite recipes.

Tansy (Tanacetum vulgare)

CHAPTER SIX

FRIENDS' FAVOURITES

Since I was writing a book which was to be full of flower designs, I considered that it would be a thoughtful gesture to ask friends to request their favourite flowers. Some of their requests appear in projects elsewhere in this book, but three popular flowers seemed to lend themselves to small circular designs suitable for box tops.

POPULAR FLOWERS

The large-flowered *Anemone* 'De Caen' – the much-loved poppy anemone, is a favourite of Pauline, a neighbour of ours. For my last birthday, she and her husband Tony bought me a lovely terracotta bowl containing a number of anemone corms, to grow in our verandah. I followed the instructions for planting and early care, and was rewarded in the spring with a lovely bowl of red, cerise, purple and mauve blooms. The vividness of the red ones was accentuated by a white circlet surrounding their dark centres. Their foliage, too, was very attractive. Like their wild cousin, the pasqueflower, they had a whorl of three feathery leaves below the base of their flowers, as well as larger feathery leaves at the base of each plant.

While anemones are admired for their bold and beautiful colours, freesias are loved for their exquisite perfume and delicate looks. These flowers are the favourite of our friend Jenny, from 'The Queen's Armes' hotel, Charmouth, in Dorset. These fragrant flowers are often chosen for bridal bouquets and, because they come in a wide variety of colours – reds, pinks, mauves, yellow, cream and white – they will fit comfortably into any colour scheme. In a vase, they fill a room with delicate fragrance, and even in the winter months they bring a touch of spring to the home.

My third design in this chapter is of the cymbidium orchid, a lovely flower, and the choice of my friend Betty. These exotic plants originate from the Himalayan foothills, from south-eastern Asia and Australia. Most of the cymbidium hybrids available today have been bred from species originating in the region of the Himalayas. Now there are over a thousand to choose from. The flowers of these plants are long-lasting even when cut, sturdy, and sometimes highly scented. Flowers come in shades of cream, pale green, pink, salmon, red and maroon. The lip of the flower is often vividly patterned, since this is the landing platform for pollinators and must, therefore, catch their attention. The rest of the flower is less strongly marked, though often delicately shaded or striped.

These designs, made to fill a circular aperture, can also be used in greetings cards, to celebrate a birthday, or to wish someone a speedy recovery from an illness. They could also be mounted in coasters, or used on pot pourri sachets, square needlecases or pincushions – in fact, on any small, round or square gift you can devise.

Poppy anemone (Anemone 'De Caen')

THREE TRINKET BOXES

YOU WILL NEED

*The finished freesia and anemone embroideries
measure 10cm (4in) in diameter;
the finished orchid embroidery
measures 7cm (3in).*

❧ For the two larger boxes: 15cm (6in)
squares of cream 18-count Aida fabric. For
the smaller box: 12.5cm (5in) square of cream
18-count Aida fabric

❧ No 26 tapestry needle

❧ Stranded embroidery cotton in the colours
given in the panel

❧ 3 squares of iron-on interfacing,
corresponding to the sizes of the pieces of
Aida fabric

❧ Boxes of appropriate sizes, see page 127
for suppliers

THE EMBROIDERY

Find the centre point on your square of
Aida fabric and, beginning from the centre
of the chart, embroider the flower motif,
using two strands of cotton in the needle for
both the cross stitch and the backstitch.

Steam press the embroidery on the
wrong side when complete.

ASSEMBLING THE TRINKET BOXES

Iron the interfacing to the back of the
embroidery. Take the acetate inset from the
lid and place it over the embroidery. This
will enable you to centre the motif within
the circular space available. Using the
acetate as a template, draw around it with a
soft pencil. Cut around the circle with a
sharp pair of scissors, and complete the
assembly, following the manufacturer's
instructions.

Poppy anemones (Anemone 'De Caen')

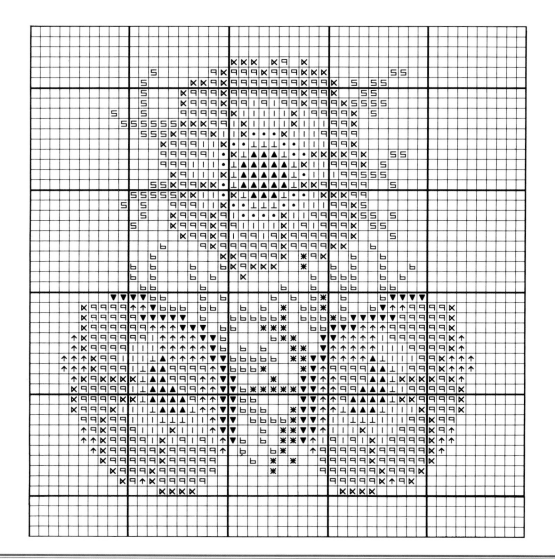

*K*EY TO CHART – *A*NEMONES

		DMC	Anchor	Madeira			DMC	Anchor	Madeira
⊥	Grey	413	401	1713	⊔	Light green	3347	267	1408
•	Ecru	Ecru	926	Ecru	↑	Deep cerise	917	88	0706
▲	Dark navy	939	127	1009	⊓	Deep pink	3607	87	0708
▼	Red	915	89	0705	⋉	Pink	3608	86	0709
✳	Dark green	3345	268	1406	❘	Pale pink	3609	85	0710
⊐	Green	3346	817	1407					

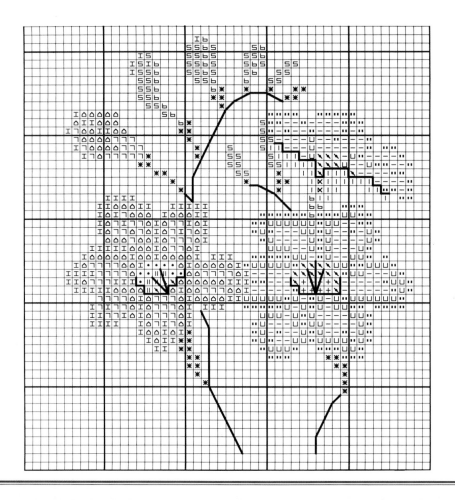

Key to Chart – Freesias

		DMC	Anchor	Madeira			DMC	Anchor	Madeira
•	Cream	746	275	0101	△	Lilac	209	109	0803
⇖	Yellow	743	297	0113	⅂	Pale lilac	210	108	0802
‖	Lemon	744	301	0112	⋈	Dark salmon pink	351	328	0214
▪▪	Light maroon	815	43	0513	I	Salmon pink	352	9	0303
⊔	Red	321	47	0510		Grey*	413	401	1713
–	Light red	349	46	0212					
✳	Dark green	3346	817	1407					
⅁	Green	3347	266	1408					
⊔	Pale green	3348	265	1409					
+	Yellow-brown	729	890	2209					
I	Deep lilac	208	110	0804					

NOTE Backstitch the stamens of the freesias in cream; the lower edge of the two flower centres in grey*; the flower stalks in dark green; and the edge of the petal of the upper flower in light maroon (*used for backstitch only).

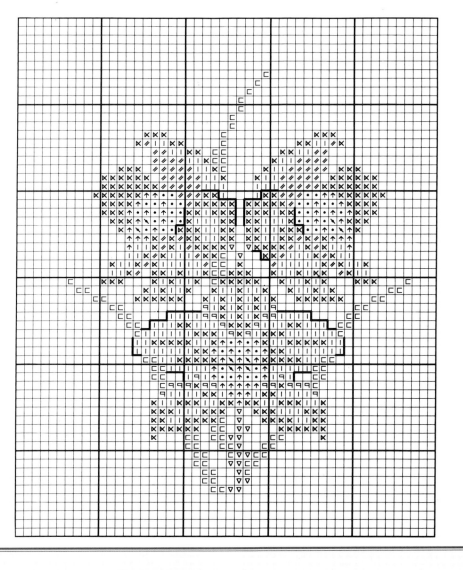

KEY TO CHART – ORCHIDS

		DMC	Anchor	Madeira
•	Ecru	Ecru	926	Ecru
↘	Yellow	743	297	0113
⁄⁄	Light red	3350	42	0603
⊏	Green	3346	817	1407
▽	Light green	3347	267	1408
↑	Maroon	814	44	0514

		DMC	Anchor	Madeira
⊓	Purplish-pink	3687	68	0604
⋉	Dusky pink	3688	66	0605
I	Pale pink	3689	49	0607

NOTE Backstitch the two petals of the lower flower in dusky pink; and the petals of each of the upper flowers in light red.

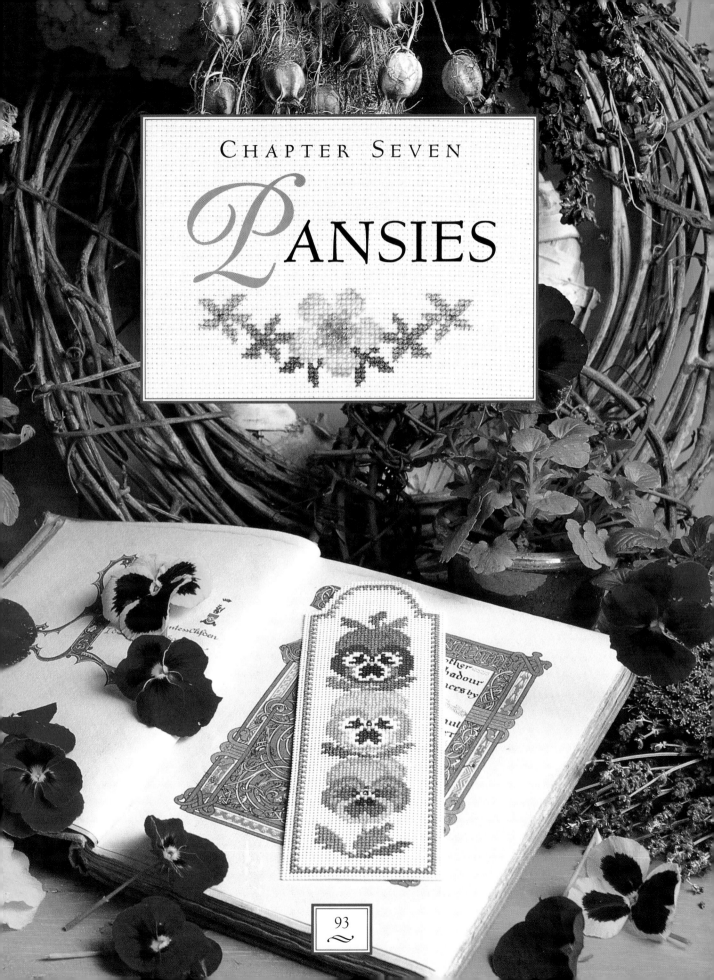

CHAPTER SEVEN

PANSIES

ANSIES, with their expressive 'faces', sometimes bright and alert, sometimes full of concentration, sometimes with a whiskery smile and sometimes sad, have endeared themselves to gardeners for generations. The pansy must be one of the best-loved and most versatile of all garden flowers. It will grow in almost any soil, and in a sunny position or in dappled shade. It is equally at home in garden borders, in planters, in pots or in hanging baskets. There are heat-tolerant varieties which produce fresh, colourful flowers, month after month throughout the summer, and there are cold-resistant varieties, which will give bright, cheerful colour during the most miserable winter months. Some of the charming small-flowered varieties grow happily in the rockery or make a pretty border along garden paths. The larger varieties make a colourful edging around beds of roses or other shrubs, which flower only for relatively short periods.

The wild pansy (*Viola tricolor*) is the beautiful little flower from which the garden pansy was bred. Since the 16th century it has been known as heartsease – a name used by Shakespeare. It has also been referred to as love-in-idleness and St Valentine's flower. The theme of love running through the many common names for the wild and garden pansy has its origin in

Pansies (Viola *sp.*)

the French word *pensée*, meaning 'thought' which, inevitably, has become associated with love, and from which the name 'pansy' is derived.

PANSY 'FACES'

The inspiration for this design came from a most attractive seed catalogue, which arrived earlier this year with our weekly gardening magazine. On the front cover of the seed catalogue was featured one of the most beautiful photographs of pansy 'faces' I have ever seen. The photograph was to celebrate the pansy as being the nation's most widely-sown flower seed.

I chose a selection of pansy 'faces', which I thought formed an attractive group. I was particularly enchanted by the puzzled frowns of 'Joker' and 'Artemis'. Joker, with its large, round, pale-blue head, deeper blue and white face and clear yellow eye, is a particular favourite of mine. Artemis has a similar expression. It was named after the Greek goddess of nature and has a large, dark violet head, deep purple and white face, and yellow eye. It will bring a wry smile and a touch of humour in the winter, when there is little else in the garden to cheer you up.

I have had to cheat a little with the other pansies, because, as avid gardeners may rightly point out, it would be difficult to get all these different varieties of pansy to flower together. I must crave a little artistic licence in order to combine my favourite pansy faces on a single panel!

VARYING THE DESIGN

The pansy picture design is ideal for a relatively small picture, though you could make it larger by working it on a 14-count fabric, but if you wanted a long, narrow panel to fill a space somewhere in your home, you could repeat the design more than once. As long as you keep the eyes of the three central pansies directly in line under one another, you can repeat the design as many times as you wish to fill the space. You may want to keep each motif of seven pansies separate from the next, by leaving a clear gap between. Alternatively you may wish to create a continuous 'panel of pansies' effect

by tucking the top blue pansy of the second motif closely under the leaves of the bottom purple pansy of the first motif.

For the bookmark, I extracted three pansy heads. It occurred to me that the pansy design is almost as versatile as the plant itself. By taking one or more flowers, together with a leaf or two, you could work a design to fit any birthday card, anniversary card, get-well card or place-setting card you choose. Individual pansy heads could be worked on table linen, or on pot pourri sacks, needlecases or other small gifts. The pansy heads could also be adapted to create a colourful border around a cushion or around a cover for a book or large folder. Just let your imagination run riot, like the flowers of the pansy plant itself!

Pansies (Viola *sp.*)

Pansy Picture

You Will Need

The finished framed picture measures 29cm x 16.5cm (11½ in x 6½ in).

- 38cm x 24cm (15in x 9½ in) of 18-count cream Aida fabric
- No 26 tapestry needle
- Stranded embroidery cotton in the colours given in the panel
- 12.5cm x 25cm (5in x 10in) of strong card, for mounting the embroidery
- Strong thread, for lacing the embroidery over the card
- Frame of your choice

THE EMBROIDERY

Find the centre point on your piece of Aida fabric and, beginning from the centre of the chart, work all cross stitch using two strands of cotton in the needle. Then add the back-stitch, for which two strands of cotton in the needle are also required.

Steam press the finished embroidery on the wrong side.

MOUNTING & FRAMING

Mark the centre of the card and align this with the centre of the embroidery. Lace the embroidery over the card following the instructions on page 126.

Complete the assembly of the frame according to the manufacturer's instructions.

Key to Chart – Pansy Picture

		DMC	Anchor	Madeira
•	White	Blanc	1	White
Z	Deep yellow	742	303	0107
➘	Yellow	743	297	0113
‖	Lemon	745	300	0111
┳	Dark navy	939	127	1009
▲	Navy	823	150	1008
△	Azure blue	799	130	0910
✕	Blue	794	175	0907
◇	Pale blue	800	129	0909
▐▐	Maroon	902	72	0601
▽	Deep violet	552	101	0713
—	Violet	553	98	0712
⊏	Dark green	3345	268	1406
▽	Light green	3347	267	1408
⊔	Yellow-green	471	266	1501
⅃	Deep purple	550	102	0714
⊥	Deep lilac	208	111	0804
⌂	Lilac	209	109	0803
⅂	Pale lilac	210 .	108	0802
↑	Dull purple	327	100	0805

NOTE Backstitch the pansy centres in dark navy.

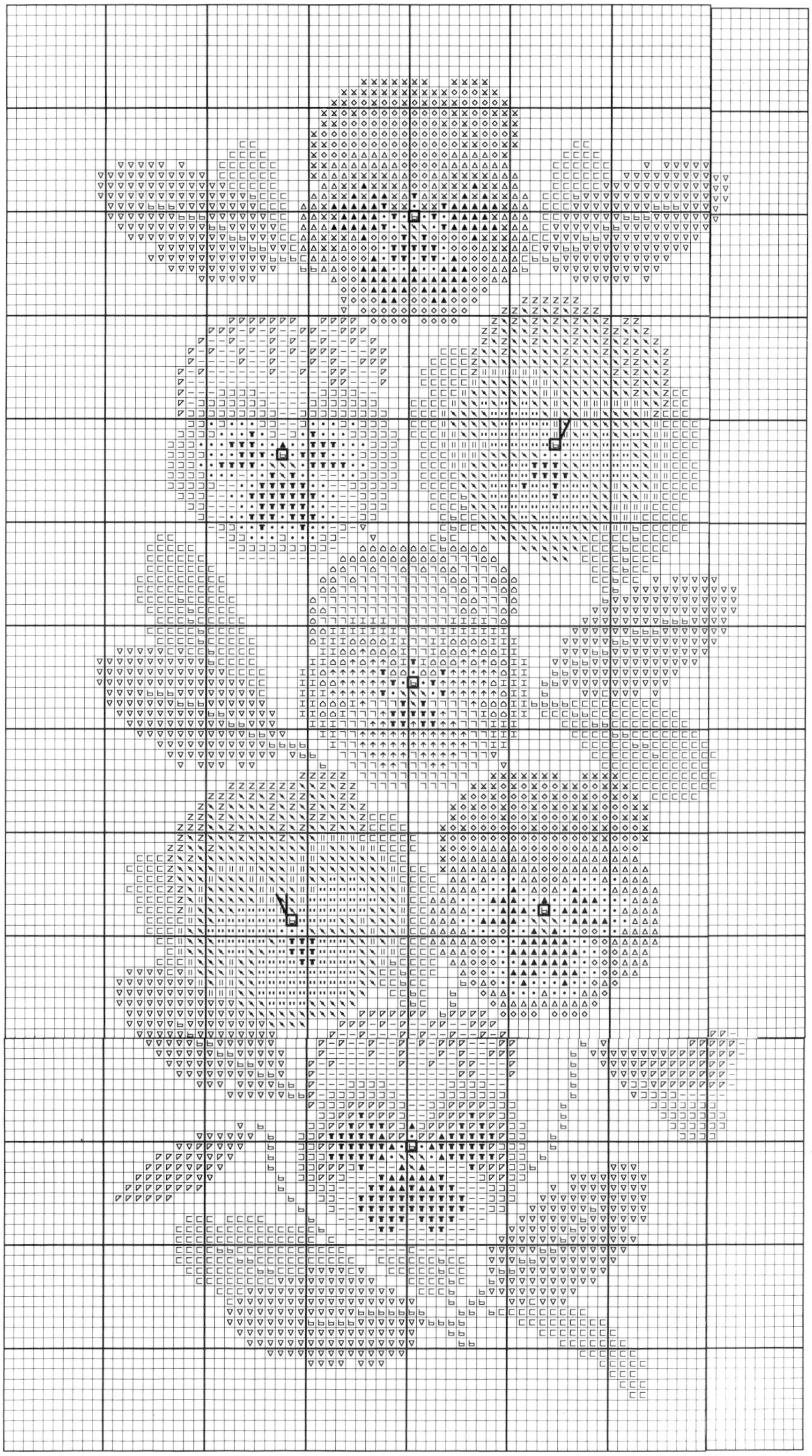

𝒫ANSY BOOKMARK

THE EMBROIDERY

Find the centre of the paper by counting the spaces between the holes. Find the centre of the chart and begin at this point. Use three strands of cotton in the needle for both the cross stitch and the backstitch.

FINISHING THE BOOKMARK

Centre the iron-on interfacing on the wrong side of the embroidered paper. Iron it into place.

Trim around the border of the design, leaving an edging of two perforations. You may find it easier to mark your cutting line with a soft pencil before cutting. If you like, you could trim the bookmark with a ribbon for a finishing touch.

Pansies (Viola sp.)

Key to Chart – Pansy Bookmark

		DMC	Anchor	Madeira
•	White	Blanc	1	White
❨	Yellow	743	297	0113
T	Dark navy	939	127	1009
▲	Navy	823	150	1008
△	Azure blue	799	130	0910
✕	Blue	794	175	0907
◇	Pale blue	800	129	0909
▽	Deep violet	552	101	0713
–	Violet	553	98	0712
⊏	Dark green	3345	268	1406
S	Green	3346	817	1407
⊔	Yellow-green	471	266	1501
⊐	Deep purple	550	102	0714
I	Deep lilac	208	111	0804
⌂	Lilac	209	109	0803
⊓	Pale lilac	210	108	0802
↑	Dull purple	327	100	0805

Note Backstitch the pansy centres in dark navy.

CHAPTER EIGHT

TROPICAL FLORA

THE YEARS I SPENT TEACHING in Jamaica, at St Hilda's High School in Brown's Town, were very special years. Brown's Town lies in a craggy limestone hollow, surrounded by high, shrub-covered plateau land. Twelve kilometres to the north lies the coastal plain, with its lush green fields of sugar cane. About 80 kilometres to the south-east lies Kingston, while about 65 kilometres to the west lies the well-known holiday centre of Montego Bay. The variety of tropical scenery, the climate, the people and their customs, the fauna, and above all the flora were all totally different from anything that I had experienced before.

Around the front courtyard of the school, just as the land fell away precipitously down to the school playing fields and the market town beyond, the poinciana trees were afire with their flame-coloured flowers for much of the year. At the back of the school hall, sky-blue plumbago flowered. The dazzling purples, pinks and reds of the bougainvillea, the fragrant pink flowers of the frangipani or West Indian jasmine, and the mauve-blue of the petrea which climbed up the wall of the headteacher's flat, were all a feast for the eyes. Every plant had its season for flowering, but there was never a time when it was impossible to find flowers blooming. Indeed it was a custom at St Hilda's, which was a boarding school, that every table should be decorated with a vase of fresh flowers at mealtimes.

TROPICAL TABLECLOTH

When I set myself the task of creating a tropical design for a tablecloth, I had a vision of a cloth covered in bright and colourful flowers but, on reflection, I thought that this might be too vivid for most people's taste. Nevertheless, I decided on red for the dominant colour – since this reflects the warm and extrovert personality of the tropics. I decided on two flowers, each of which reminds me of two very dear Jamaican friends of mine.

The hibiscus (*Hibiscus rosa-sinensis*) is for Vi Parke, the school secretary of St Hilda's, who took me under her wing from the moment I stepped off the boat in Kingston. This particular hibiscus is native of China, where it has been cultivated for centuries, but now it grows throughout the tropics. The shrubs grow from only 90cm (36in) to 2.6m (3yd) tall. The flowers come in a wide variety of shades of red, salmon pink, rose pink, cream and yellow. Some plants produce single, some double and some triple flowers. The hibiscus flower has become synonymous with the tropics, and is probably the best-known of tropical plants. The disappointing thing about these lovely blooms, however, is that they only live for a day – or two if you are very lucky.

My first encounter with hibiscuses growing as garden flowers, was when Vi took me up to her home at Golden Hill, in the foothills of the Blue Mountains, behind Kingston. Here hibiscuses grew in abundance, and I remember being shown how to clear the weeds, plant and prune the shrubs Jamaican fashion – with a machete! Vi also liked to take me for drives along the north coast of the island. Here hibiscus shrubs formed high hedges between the modest one-storey homes constructed of wood and corrugated iron. There was every colour of hibiscus imaginable, and it was on one of these outings that I saw a shrub of *Hibiscus schizopetalus* – a particularly beautiful plant, native to East Africa, whose pendulous flowers have elegantly cut and fringed petals – a real challenge to any designer of cross stitch, but a challenge I should like to take up one day. For this cloth, however, I contented myself with a single-petalled red *Hibiscus rosa-sinensis*.

The second flower I chose for this design is the gloriosa lily (*Gloriosa superba*). It has large, vividly-coloured, orange-red and yellow flowers. It is a peculiar lily in that it is a herbaceous climber, ascending by means of the leaves which have twining tendril tips. The petals look as if they are being blown backwards in the wind, and their edges are delicately waved.

It was Lorna Walder, the House Mother at St Hilda's, who first introduced me to these lovely flowers. At weekends, when she was not on duty in school, she would take me to her home at Walderston, near Mandeville. Lorna knew not only the common name but also the botanical name of every flower I encountered on the island. Her garden was full of flowers, and our task, before returning to school on a Sunday night, was to gather armfuls of blooms and cram them into vases and buckets of water. There were yellow day lilies, pink hippeastrum lilies, red and yellow heliconia, pink periwinkle, blue plumbago, red anthuriums, deep orange ground orchids, and many more. The various receptacles were then carefully loaded into Lorna's old black Ford Prefect and, with flowers poking through every open window, we set off back to school.

Sunday nights were spent arranging flowers in vases for the school hall, chapel, head-teacher's office and flat, and the staff room. Pride of place, I remember, was always given to the lovely gloriosa lilies which, even in Lorna's garden, were always rather rare and special flowers.

VARYING THE DESIGN

In my design, the hibiscus and the gloriosa lily form a circular design which could be worked on any size of square tablecloth. On a larger cloth you may like to work a single hibiscus flower or a gloriosa lily in each corner, in addition to the circular motif. On an oblong cloth you may wish to do more than one circular design. You may also like to embroider matching napkins made in the same material as the cloth, and with a single flower on each. However you decide to use the design, I hope it will bring a touch of the tropics into your home.

Hibiscus (Hibiscus rosa-sinensis)

ℐHE TABLECLOTH

𝒴OU WILL NEED

The tablecloth can be any size you wish, as long as it is square. The tablecloth illustrated here measures 80cm (31½in) square. The circle of embroidered flowers measures 40.5cm x 40.5cm (16in x 16in) in diameter.

- ❧ 1m (40in) square of 27/28-count Linda fabric
- ❧ No 24 tapestry needle
- ❧ Stranded embroidery cotton in the colours given in the panel
- ❧ Matching cotton

THE EMBROIDERY

Find the centre of your square of fabric and mark it with basting stitches. From this point count 118 threads to the left, and this will bring you to the upper tip of the gloriosa petal. Using three strands of cotton in the needle, and working over two threads of the fabric, work the three stitches in dark red. This will establish the starting place for your embroidery. Work the design flower by flower, completing the backstitch using three strands of cotton in the needle. By doing this you will find it easier to count the number of threads between one flower and the next. It is crucial that this counting is

done accurately otherwise your circle of blooms will not join up!

FINISHING THE TABLECLOTH

This can be done in one of three ways. You can hem stitch a narrow hem on all sides, machine the hem on all sides, or make a fringe on all sides.

The cloth illustrated here has a hand-sewn hem stitch edging on all sides. Gently steam press the finished tablecloth on the wrong side.

The chart for the tablecloth has been split over four pages. Refer to this diagram to check the relevant page on which each section of the chart falls.

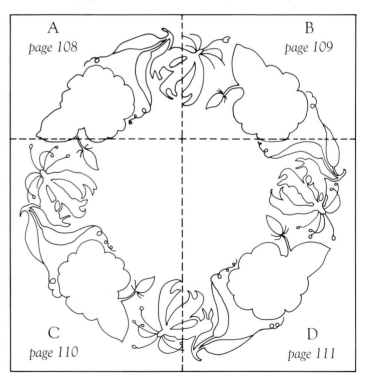

A
page 108

B
page 109

C
page 110

D
page 111

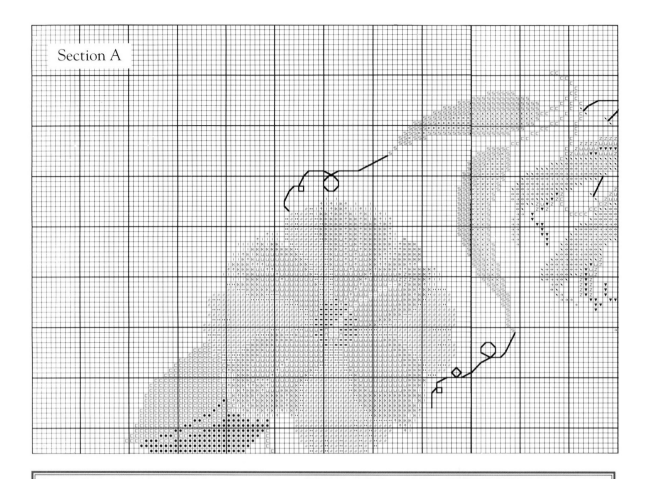

Section A

$\mathcal{K}$EY TO CHART – $\mathcal{T}$ABLECLOTH

		DMC	Anchor	Madeira
⊓	Black	310	403	Black
▬	Maroon	814	44	0514
Z	Gold	972	298	0107
↘	Yellow	973	290	0105
▼	Deep red	816	799	0512
❙❙	Light maroon	815	43	0513
⁄⁄	Dull red	347	13	0407
⊔	Light red	349	46	0212
−	Pink	353	8	0304
→	Dark red	498	19	0511
⊹	Orange-red	606	335	0209
●	Dark blue-green	3345	263	1406

		DMC	Anchor	Madeira
⊏	Green	3346	817	1407
⊐	Dark lime green	469	268	1503
⊔	Lime green	470	267	1502
÷	Light green	3347	261	1408
K	Pale green	471	266	1501
↑	Deep salmon	351	10	0214
⋈	Deep pink	350	11	0213
I	Light salmon	352	9	0303

NOTE Backstitch the stamens of the gloriosa in lime green; the pistil of the gloriosa and the base of the hibiscus bud in dark blue-green; and the tendrils on the gloriosa leaves in dark lime green.

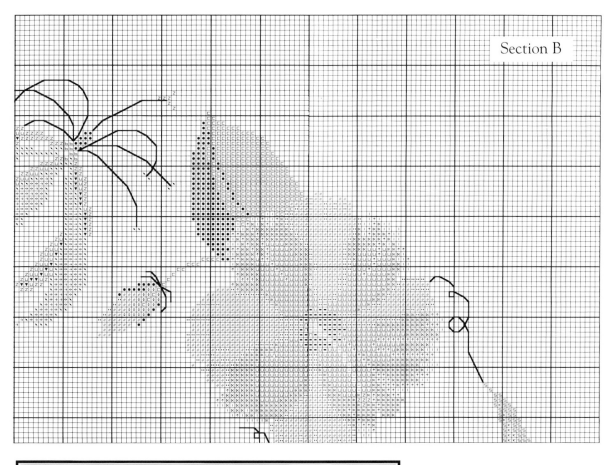

Section B

Lily (Gloriosa superba)

Section C

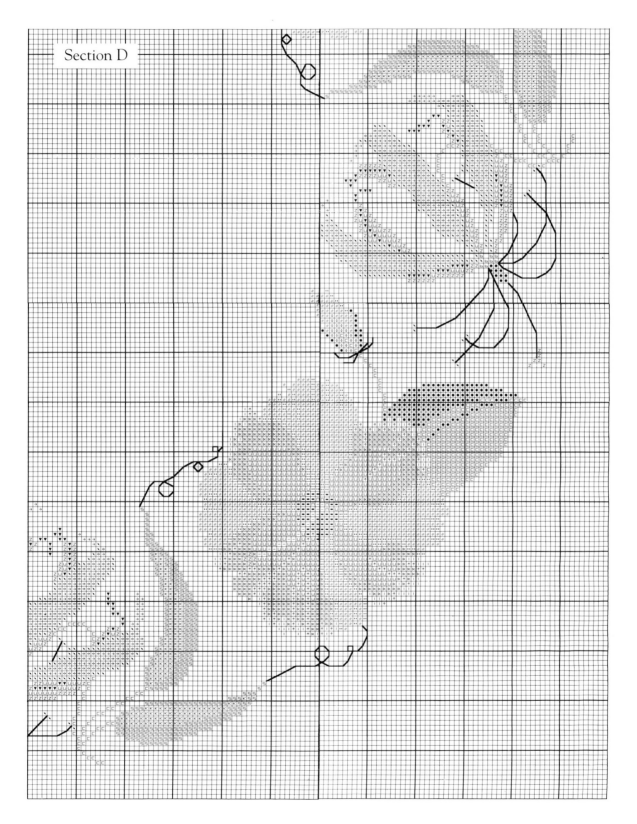

Section D

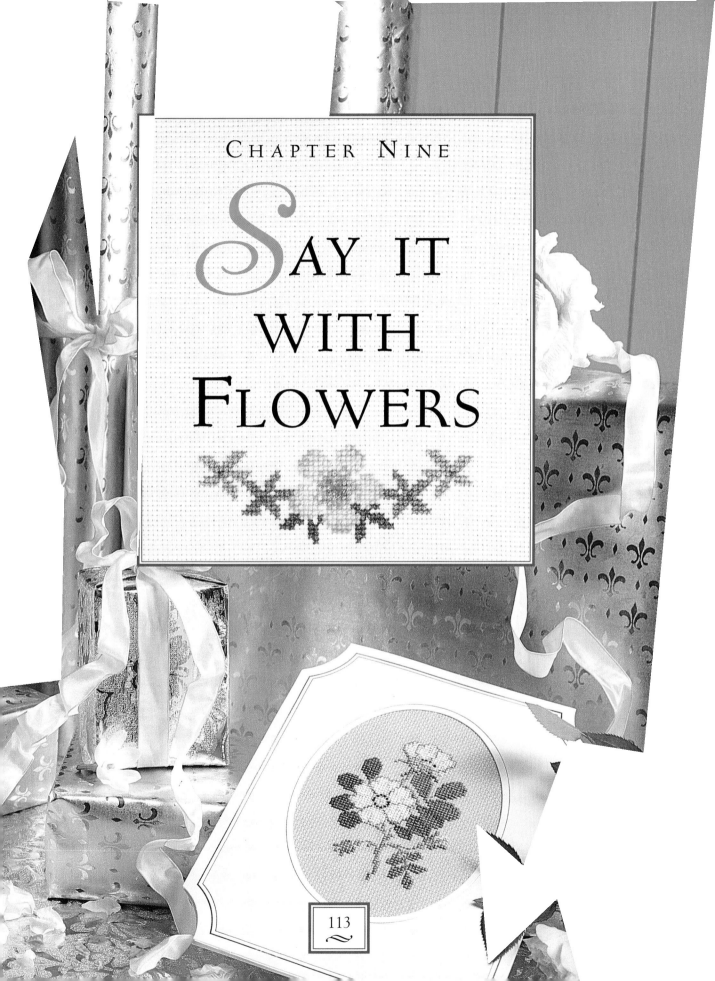

CHAPTER NINE

SAY IT WITH FLOWERS

THE ROSE IS A FLOWER most often associated with love, birthdays, weddings and other special anniversaries. The Ancient Greeks and Romans used the petals for perfume, and spread them on the floors of their homes. The thorn is said to resemble a dog's canine tooth. According to Pliny, a Roman soldier when bitten by a rabid dog applied an infusion made with the roots of a rose to heal it. Hence the wild dog rose (*Rosa canina*) got its name. It was from these wild species that all our modern roses have been bred – from the simple, elegant species roses, through the vigorous, old-fashioned shrub roses, to the modern, full-blown, hybrid tea roses, the strong climbers and the tiny, perfect miniature roses. In the Middle Ages, when the garden rose was named 'Flos Florum' (Flower of Flowers), it became the symbol of earthly and heavenly perfection. In all its lovely forms a rose brings happiness and uplifts the spirit of any garden lover.

My particular favourites are the species roses, which most resemble the wild roses. It is probably the simple beauty of their single flowers, their dainty foliage and, in autumn, their colourful hips, in a wide range of shapes and sizes, that make them so attractive.

ROSE DESIGNS

For the silver wedding card I have chosen *Rosa rugosa alba*. The lovely, single, white flowers have a pure, silky texture. They are larger than, but otherwise very similar to, the wild field rose (*Rosa arvensis*). The roses are quickly followed by large, orange-red hips. To make the white rose design appropriate for a silver wedding celebration, I have used some silver blending filament. I used Kreinik thread, but if this is not available, there are other fine, silver, metallic threads on the market which should work equally well. The same design can also be used to make a pearl wedding card for a 30th wedding anniversary. Use a pearly or opalescent blending filament in place of the silver one. You can also adapt the design for a diamond wedding, celebrating 60 years of marriage. Keep the silver blending thread, and add tiny, sparkling diamante stones to the centre of the rose, or stick some carefully on the tips of the leaves to look like raindrops. You can buy packets of these stones in many needlework and craft shops.

For the ruby wedding card, I chose the species rose, *Rosa moyesii*. In our garden, it

Species rose (Rosa moyesii)

has grown into a beautiful monster of a rose bush, which looks somewhere between a shrub and a climber! Its foliage is like that of a rather sophisticated dog rose, and the shape of its flowers also reflects its origins. The colour, however, is stunning – rich purplish-red, accentuated, when the flower first comes out, by a gold circlet of stamens. In a day or two the stamens turn golden-brown, and the pale green centre becomes

Rosa rugosa alba

more prominent. The flowers appear from mid-summer onwards, and when these are finished we look forward to seeing the shiny, flagon-shaped hips, which turn a vivid orange-red in the autumn. The tall, sturdy, spreading stems of the shrub fan out to make a perfect climbing frame for our wide-ranging grey squirrels who seem quite oblivious of the vicious thorns growing closely along every branch.

In my design for the golden wedding card I have used *Rosa x* 'Canary Bird'. This rose also seems to do well in our garden, growing vigorously and arching over the roof of our garden shed. The small, fern-like leaves of this rose are very delicate and attractive, and its cupped flowers which measure 5cm (2in) across, have a musky scent. The roses appear in late spring, when they cover the shrub with a mass of bright, cheerful, yellow blooms. In autumn there are sometimes one or two late flowers before

the shrub finally goes into hibernation for the winter. In this design, I thought it appropriate to use a gold blending filament to give the embroidery a sparkle. Again, I used Kreinik thread, but if you have difficulty in obtaining this, there are several other suitable brands of gold metallic thread on the market.

Since there is quite a lot of work in these designs and you may not want to expend so much energy on making something as ephemeral as a greetings card, why not include with the card an appropriate frame, into which the recipients can mount their picture when the card has served its purpose? You may like to work the design on a more useful reminder of the special day. For example, a set of place mats and matching serviettes would make a memorable gift for the home.

Three Greetings Cards

You Will Need

The silver and gold wedding anniversary cards measure approximately 20cm x 14.5cm (8in x 5¾in) with an aperture of 12.5cm x 9cm (5in x 3½in). The ruby wedding anniversary card measures 20cm x 15cm (8in x 6in) with an aperture of 14.5cm x 9.5cm (5¾in x 3¾in).

❧ For the golden wedding anniversary card: 20cm x 15cm (8in x 6in) of 18-count cream Aida fabric

❧ For the ruby anniversary card: 20cm x 15cm (8in x 6in) of 18-count cream Aida fabric

❧ For the silver wedding anniversary card: 20cm x 15cm (8in x 6in) of 18-count slate grey Aida fabric

❧ No 26 tapestry needle

❧ Stranded embroidery cotton in the colours given in the panel

❧ For each card: 20cm x 15cm (8in x 6in) iron-on interfacing

THE EMBROIDERY

Find the centre point on your Aida fabric and, beginning from the centre of the chart, work all cross stitches using two strands of cotton in the needle. Where a blending filament is indicated, use one strand of cotton together with one strand of metallic blending thread.

Complete your design by adding the backstitch, using two strands of cotton.

Carefully steam press your embroidery on the wrong side, using a cloth to avoid direct contact between iron and metallic thread.

MAKING UP THE CARDS

Iron the interfacing on to the back of the embroidery, and trim both to about 12mm (½in) larger all around than the card aperture. This will help to prevent the mounted picture from wrinkling.

I have mounted my ruby wedding card so that the threads run at 45 degrees to the horizontal. You may like to use this method for either of the other two cards, or you may prefer to mount them straight in the usual way.

Position the embroidery behind the aperture. Fold the card and press firmly to secure it if it is self-adhesive. Some cards are not self-adhesive and will require a dab of glue to ensure a neat and secure finish.

Dog rose (Rosa canina)

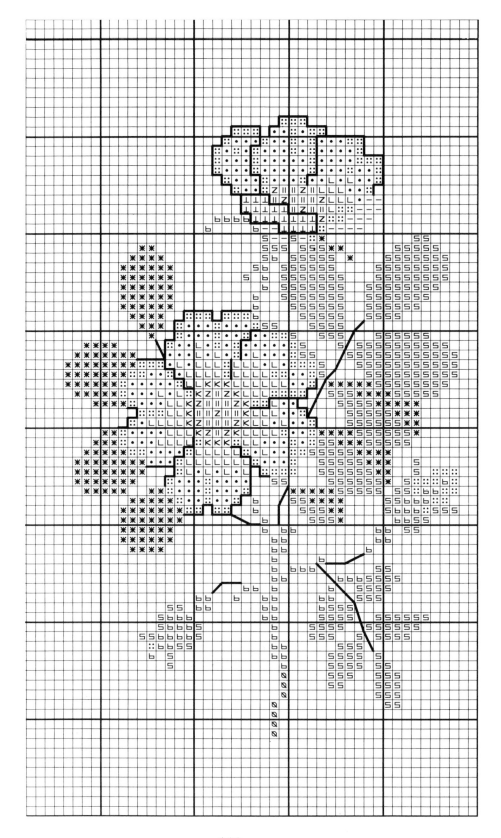

KEY TO CHART – SILVER WEDDING CARD

		DMC	Anchor	Madeira			DMC	Anchor	Madeira
⊥	Pale grey	318	399	1802	⊠ Light brown		611	898	2107
∶∶	White & silver	Blanc	1	White + Kreinik	Dark grey*		413	401	1713
				blending filament	Grey*		414	400	1801
•	White	Blanc	1	White	Dark brown*		3371	382	2004
∟	Ecru	Ecru	926	Ecru					
Z	Deep yellow	742	303	0107					
‖	Lemon	727	293	0110					
—	Pale pink	963	23	0608					
✳	Dark green	3345	268	1406					
5	Green	3346	817	1407					
┗	Light green	3347	267	1408					
K	Pale green	3348	265	1409					

NOTE Backstitch the leaf and bud stalks in light green; the stitches separating the petals near the centre of the lower rose in dark grey*; and the outline of the petals on both roses in grey* (*used for backstitch or french knots only). Work five french knots over the centre of the top rose and twelve french knots around the centre of the lower rose in dark brown. (For the sake of clarity these have not been shown on the chart.)

Rosa 'Canary Bird'

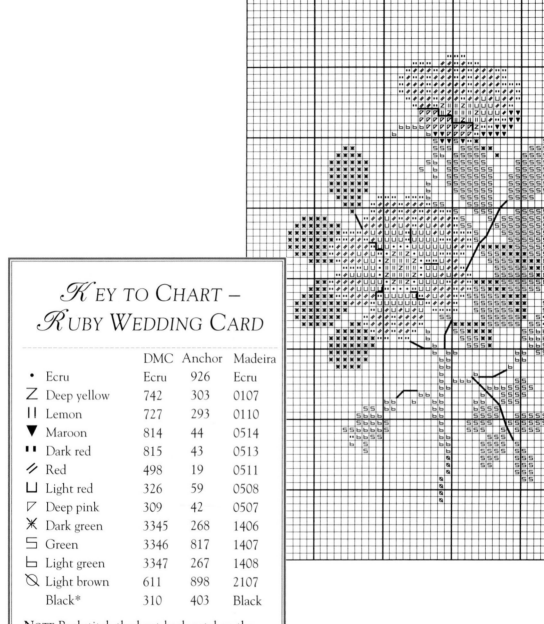

𝒦EY TO CHART – 𝓡UBY WEDDING CARD

		DMC	Anchor	Madeira
•	Ecru	Ecru	926	Ecru
Z	Deep yellow	742	303	0107
‖	Lemon	727	293	0110
▼	Maroon	814	44	0514
▪▪	Dark red	815	43	0513
∥	Red	498	19	0511
Ц	Light red	326	59	0508
▽	Deep pink	309	42	0507
✳	Dark green	3345	268	1406
ᒣ	Green	3346	817	1407
ᒧ	Light green	3347	267	1408
◹	Light brown	611	898	2107
	Black*	310	403	Black

NOTE Backstitch the bent-back petal on the upper rose in maroon; the leaf and bud stalks in light green; and the stitches separating the petals near the centre of the lower rose in black* (*used for backstitch only). Work five french knots over the centre of the top rose and twelve french knots around the centre of the lower rose in maroon. (For the sake of clarity these have not been shown on the chart.)

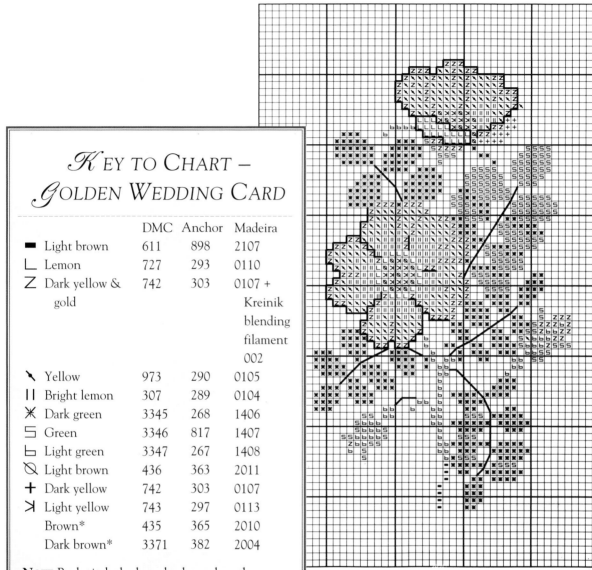

Key to Chart – Golden Wedding Card

	DMC	Anchor	Madeira
▬ Light brown	611	898	2107
L Lemon	727	293	0110
Z Dark yellow & gold	742	303	0107 + Kreinik blending filament 002
↘ Yellow	973	290	0105
‖ Bright lemon	307	289	0104
✳ Dark green	3345	268	1406
⊑ Green	3346	817	1407
⊔ Light green	3347	267	1408
◙ Light brown	436	363	2011
+ Dark yellow	742	303	0107
⋋ Light yellow	743	297	0113
Brown*	435	365	2010
Dark brown*	3371	382	2004

NOTE Backstitch the bent-back petal on the upper rose in brown*; the outline of petals on the lower rose and the highest petals of the upper rose in light brown; the bud stalk in light green; the rib of the top right-hand leaf in green; the ribs of the other leaves in dark green; and the stitches separating the petals near the centre of the lower rose in dark brown* (*used for backstitch or french knots only). Work five french knots over the centre of the top rose and twelve french knots around the centre of the lower rose in dark brown. (For the sake of clarity these have not been shown on the chart.)

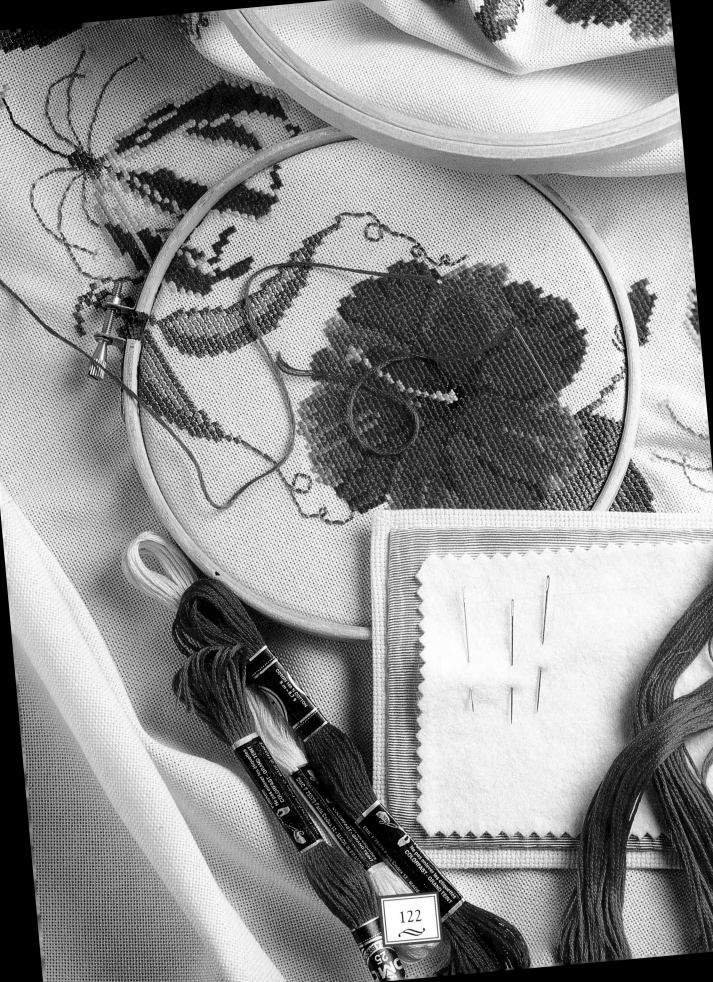

CROSS STITCH

BASIC TECHNIQUES

PREPARING THE FABRIC

Even with an average amount of handling, many evenweave fabrics tend to fray at the edges, so it is a good idea to overcast the raw edges, using ordinary sewing thread, before you begin.

THE INSTRUCTIONS

Each project begins with a full list of the materials that you will require: Aida and Linda fabrics are produced by Zweigart. Note that the measurements given for the embroidery fabric include a minimum of 3cm (1¼in) all around to allow for preparing the edges to prevent them from fraying.

Colour keys for stranded embroidery cottons – DMC, Anchor or Madeira – are given with each chart. It is assumed that you will need to buy one skein of each colour mentioned in a particular key, even though you may use less, but where two or more skeins are needed, this information is included in the main list of requirements.

To work from the charts, particularly those where several symbols are used in close proximity, some readers may find it helpful to have the chart enlarged so that the squares and symbols can be seen more easily. Many photocopying services will do this for a minimum charge.

Before you begin to embroider, always mark the centre of the design with two lines of basting stitches, one vertical and one horizontal, running from edge to edge of the fabric, as indicated by the arrows on the charts.

As you stitch, use the centre lines given on the chart and the basting threads on your fabric as reference points for counting the squares and threads to position your design accurately.

Cross stitch

To make a cross stitch, bring the needle up from the back of the material at the point at which you wish to begin. Carefully hold the end of the thread as you pull your needle through, and secure the loose end with your first five or six stitches. Never begin with a knot.

For a single cross stitch, as shown below, bring the needle up at 1, down at 2, up at 3 and down at 4.

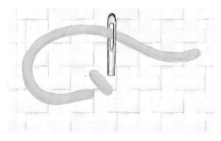

For stitching rows of cross stitch – stitch all the way across, making a row of diagonal stitches, as shown, and then work back, completing each stitch in turn.

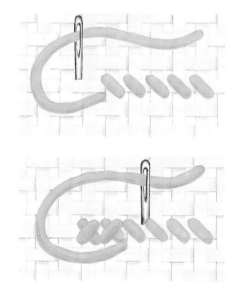

Whether you are making single cross stitches or rows of cross stitches, ensure that all stitches cross in the same direction.

Backstitch

Backstitch is used to emphasize a particular line or to add fine detail to a design. The stitches are either worked as continuous straight lines parallel with the threads of the material, or they are worked diagonally.

To make a stitch, push the needle up through the material from the back of your work and down through the fabric one stitch length behind the first point. Pass the needle under the material, and then up one stitch length ahead of the first point.

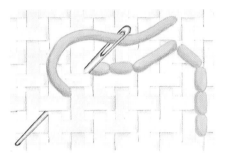

French knots

To work a french knot, bring your needle and cotton out slightly to the right of where you want your knot to be. Wind the thread once around the needle and insert the needle to the left of the point where you brought it out.

Be careful not to pull too hard or the knot will disappear through the fabric.

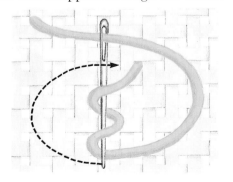

Mitring corners

Press a single hem to the wrong side, the same as the measurement given in the instructions. Open the hem out again and fold the corner of the fabric inwards as shown on the diagram. Refold the hem to the wrong side along the pressed line, and slip stitch in place.

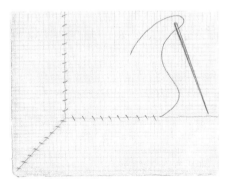

MOUNTING EMBROIDERY

The cardboard should be cut to the size of the finished embroidery, with an extra 6mm (¼in) added all around to allow for the recess in the frame.

Lightweight fabrics

1 Place the embroidery face down, with the cardboard centred on top, and basting and pencil lines matching. Begin by folding over the fabric at each corner and securing it with masking tape.

2 Working first on one side and then the other, fold over the fabric on all sides and secure it firmly with pieces of masking tape, placed about 2.5cm (1in) apart. Also neaten the mitred corners with masking tape, pulling the fabric tightly to give a firm, smooth finish.

Heavier fabrics

Lay the embroidery face down, with the cardboard centred on top; fold over the edges of the fabric on opposite sides, making mitred folds at the corners, and lace across, using strong thread. Repeat on the other two sides. Finally, pull up the stitches fairly tightly to stretch the fabric firmly over the cardboard. Overstitch the mitred corners.

ACKNOWLEDGEMENTS

I SHOULD LIKE TO THANK my mother, Violet Watts, who made up or assembled all the embroidered articles illustrated in this book, and who patiently recorded the steps she took and processes she employed for inclusion in the instructions for finishing the projects.

I should also like to thank Betty Haste for all her help in finding fresh and perfect specimens of flowers for me to work from, and for checking charts and proofs at all stages of the preparation of this book.

My thanks are also due to Pauline and Anne of the Kaleidoscope needlework and craft materials shop, The Square, Codsall, Staffordshire, who have followed the progress of this book with such interest and have always been at hand with practical help and suggestions.

For the opportunity to take photographs of many beautiful flowering plants, I would like to thank John Massey and Philip Baulk of Ashwood Nurseries, Kingswinford, West Midlands. Their enthusiasm for my designs and encouragement has been a great support to me, and the photographs have been invaluable in my work.

I should also like to say a sincere thank you to Alan Lord, Business and Personal Developments, for his advice and technical help with the transfer of my charts to computer, always given with such patience and good humour.

My acknowledgements would not be complete without a sincere thank you to Ian Lawson-Smith of IL-SOFT, Specialist Craft Software, Witney, Oxfordshire, for his help and advice concerning the use of his excellent stitch design programmes.

Finally, I must express my appreciation to friends and neighbours who followed the creation of these designs with such interest and gave me so much encouragement.

SUPPLIERS

THREADS
Coats Patons Crafts
(*Customer Liaison*)
McMullen Road,
Darlington,
Co Durham DL1 1YQ
Coats Patons Crafts will supply information regarding local stockists for Anchor stranded cottons and Kreinik metallic threads.

BOXES
Framecraft Miniatures Ltd
372/376 Summer Lane, Hockley,
Birmingham B19 3QA

MATERIALS
Poppies Needlecrafts
(Mail Order Suppliers)
1 Royal Court,
Leicester Road,
Narborough,
Leicester LE9 5EG

CLOCK
The Inglestone Collection
Milton Place,
Cirencester Road,
Fairford,
Gloucester GL7 4HR

$\mathcal{I}$NDEX